Praise
Uncensored

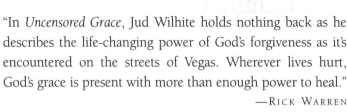

"In *Uncensored Grace*, Jud Wilhite holds nothing back as he describes the life-changing power of God's forgiveness as it's encountered on the streets of Vegas. Wherever lives hurt, God's grace is present with more than enough power to heal."

—RICK WARREN
Founding pastor of Saddleback Church and
author of *The Purpose Driven Life*

"What happens in Vegas just went public! *Uncensored Grace* is full of surprises and twists. It will captivate and inspire you as it describes the difference Jesus can make in your life."

—LEE STROBEL
Author of *The Case for Christ*

"What God is up to in Vegas is nothing short of hardcore. Jud describes an extreme faith that is extremely amazing. With clarity and passion, *Uncensored Grace* offers a renewed sense of hope for whatever you are up against. Don't miss this book."

—STEPHEN BALDWIN
Actor and author of *The Unusual Suspect*

"Jud Wilhite is a compelling new voice and model for a new way to be Christian in today's culture."

—GABE LYONS
Founder of Fermi Project and cofounder of Catalyst

"Reading *Uncensored Grace* will open your eyes to the wonders of God's saving love. It will give you hope that, no matter where you are in your 'process,' God is at work—and He is for you."

—CRAIG GROESCHEL
Pastor of Lifechurch.tv, and
author of *Chazown* and *Confessions of a Pastor*

"*Uncensored Grace* is filled with stories God must love!"

"If you've given up dreams of ever finding a genuine fresh start in your life, you ought to read this book. Real people. Real problems. Real hope. Get ready to be rocked by a fresh touch of amazing grace."

Uncensored Grace brings the brutal truth and the message of redemptive grace front and center. I was deeply moved and so inspired by these powerful and provocative stories of God's mercy. *Uncensored Grace* will transform your faith as you get a glimpse of how Jesus has set up shop on the streets of sin city.

UNCENSORED

GRACE

Stories of Hope from the
Streets of Vegas

JUD WILHITE

WITH BILL TAAFFE

MULTNOMAH
BOOKS

UNCENSORED GRACE
PUBLISHED BY MULTNOMAH BOOKS
12265 Oracle Boulevard, Suite 200
Colorado Springs, Colorado 80921

All Scripture quotations, unless otherwise noted, are taken from the Holy Bible, New International Version©. NIV ©. Copyright © 1973, 1978, 1984 by International Bible Society. Used by permission of Zondervan Publishing House. All rights reserved. Scripture quotations marked (MSG) are taken from The Message by Eugene H. Peterson. Copyright © 1993, 1994, 1995, 1996, 2000, 2001, 2002. Used by permission of NavPress Publishing Group. All rights reserved.

ISBN 978-1-60142-146-3

Published in the United States by WaterBrook Multnomah, an imprint of The Doubleday Publishing Group, a division of Random House Inc., New York.

MULTNOMAH and its mountain colophon are registered trademarks of Random House Inc.

Library of Congress Cataloging-in-Publication Data
Wilhite, Jud, 1971–
    Uncensored Grace : Stories of hope from the streets of Vegas / Jud Wilhite ; with Bill Taaffe.
        p. cm.
    1. Las Vegas (Nev.)—Religious life and customs. 2. Las Vegas (Nev.)—Church history. 3. Christian biography—Nevada—Las Vegas. 4. Christianity and culture—Nevada—Las Vegas. I. Taaffe, William. II. Title.
    BR560.L37W55 2006
    277.93'135083—dc22

                                                    2006036720

Printed in the United States of America
2009

10 9 8 7 6 5 4 3 2 1

SPECIAL SALES
Most WaterBrook Multnomah books are available in special quantity discounts when purchased in bulk by corporations, organizations, and special interest groups. Custom imprinting or excerpting can also be done to fit special needs. For information, please e-mail SpecialMarkets@WaterBrookMultnomah.com or call 1-800-603-7051.

To the Central family,
for the grace you show to so many.

Contents

About **Uncensored Grace**

U ncensored Grace is the story of a phenomenon happening
on, around, and beyond the Strip. You see, I live in the city
many experts think most symbolizes the spirit of America, if
not exactly what we are today, then certainly where we are
headed—Las Vegas.

People come here looking for something more, but what
they often find is the killing effect of unbridled pleasure,
money, and excess. Even more, they come face-to-face with
their own limits. They came here to win big, but many lose
everything. They are stripped. Then, finally, they are ready to
get honest about their lives, their faith, and their pasts. They
are, in other words, perfect candidates for uncensored grace.

Some of what Bill Taaffe and I share will shock you. Some
will surprise you. All will inspire. Why? Because each person
has, in some visceral way, been stripped of hope and human
indulgence, and with nowhere else to turn, has embraced God
with amazing passion and dramatic results.

All in one, Uncensored Grace is a portrait of eight unforget-
table people, the story of a very unique faith community, and an
inside look at the City of Entertainment. The book is organized
in four parts, each showing a different dimension of God's

love and forgiveness. At the end of each section I'll reflect on God's grace and how it has not only turned my life upside down, but how it can do the same for you.

And that brings me to one final explanation. As a pastor, I completely misjudged what grace could look like in my world. Sure, I believed in a God who passionately and persistently pursues every human being, no matter how beat up or broken. I believed, but not enough.

Not nearly.

So in addition to this book being the story of people, a church, and a city, *Uncensored Grace* is the personal confession of one who is only now beginning to see how good uncensored grace really is.

—Jud Wilhite
January 2007
Las Vegas

About the Stories

In certain cases, names have been changed in *Uncensored Grace* to protect the privacy of both the subjects of the stories and others who are mentioned. In some instances minor dialogue has been created and incidental details have been changed or assumed, usually for continuity's sake. Most details have been based on interviews with the individual subjects and, in some cases, secondary sources. Specifically, the descriptions of the adult shows in "Skin to Skin" were drawn completely from interviews with the subjects and newspaper or magazine reviews of the shows.

PART ONE: GRACE CITY

CHAPTER ONE

Viva Las Vegas

W elcome to lost wages," the flight attendant announced to laughter. "I mean…Las Vegas." As the plane landed, I was met with the sight of an Egyptian pyramid, the New York skyline, and the Eiffel Tower, all on the famous four-mile "Strip" of casinos and resorts. What could be expected, I wondered, in a place that would bring together replicas of the world's greatest wonders into one tourist circus?

Getting off the plane, I was assaulted by the nonstop clanging of airport slot machines and visual come-ons from posters of entertainers, dancers, showgirls, and comedians. We stayed in an old hotel on the Strip with popcorn-textured ceilings so low I slightly ducked while walking the halls. Everything in our hotel was dated, giving me the unique sensation of starring in a 1960s movie set in Vegas. Decades of nicotine stains seemed to ooze from the walls, but the energy was undeniable, and the people dropping coins in the slots didn't seem to mind the decor one bit.

As the sun set, I headed out of the hotel to check out the Strip. A guy on the sidewalk held out what I thought was an invitation to a concert. Instead, it was an ad for a call girl— one of several I'd be offered with each block I walked. There I stood, a pastor holding a printed sexual proposition. *Well, Dorothy, we're not in Kansas anymore.* The amazing indoor spaces at Caesars, the fountains of the Bellagio, the canals at the Venetian, the Fremont Street experience, the Stratosphere, the lights of the Strip, the mind-boggling flow of money, and the endless sea of people—it was decadent, surreal, and overwhelming...

That trip, with three coworkers, actually brought me to Vegas not to play, but for a planning retreat. Vegas was just a quick, cheap flight, and several of us had never been. Not even in my wildest dreams would I have imagined that within five years I'd actually move to Vegas to live, that I'd get used to the sound of slot machines, that entertainers pictured on posters at McCarran Airport would become my friends, and that I'd find there is so much more to Las Vegas than the Strip.

I lived in Southern California when the phone call came from a church in the Vegas Valley searching for a pastor. That afternoon I asked my wife, Lori, "How would you feel about moving to Henderson? It's this great town in Nevada, sort of near Las Vegas."

"How near Las Vegas?"

"Well...uh...okay, so it is near enough to see the Strip from your backyard, but please don't close your mind yet!"

To my surprise, she agreed to consider it.

After an extensive interview process, Lori and I, along with the people of Central Christian Church in Las Vegas, sensed it was the right move. Most of our friends were excited for us. Some of them were in shock. "Jud," they'd say, "you're a pastor, and you want to move to *Las Vegas*? Are you nuts??"

Our church in California sent us off with applause and

"Viva Las Vegas" blaring through the sound system. We loaded up our two-year-old daughter and all of our possessions for the drive across the desert. My wife was almost eight months pregnant with our second child. I still admire her courage to move to an unknown city where we didn't even have a doctor. Driving across the desert, a record heat wave with oppressive 120-degree temperatures greeted us. Let's just say that placing your wife in a situation where she is weeks from giving birth and it is 120 degrees is not the best way to win marital favor.

As we drove the freeway, I was filled with excitement at the possibilities. I'd be serving at Central Christian, following an awesome leader and friend, Gene Appel, who had led the church for many years. My mind raced with questions. *Am I crazy for relocating our family just before my wife gives birth? What are the people of the Vegas Valley really like? What is the city really about behind all the glitz? What is the perception of God and Christianity in Vegas? Man, will it always be this hot?*

I found a Starbucks in Primm, just across the Nevada state line. (There's nothing like a grande dry cappuccino when it is hot enough to cook an egg on the sidewalk.) With a mix of excitement and fear, we covered the last stretch of freeway, came through the pass, and suddenly there was the entire city. It amazes me that it is just there in the middle of nowhere, a desert island unto itself with its own culture and rules. It sits there like a massive frontier town that pops up out of the nothingness, one of the last cities in America with some semblance of the Wild West. Seeing the town appear from nowhere caused me to veer slightly out of my lane. The emotion of the move hit me like a wall. I whispered a prayer, "God, please protect my family."

The last thing I ever thought I'd become was a pastor—

and now, somehow, I was staring one of the world's toughest (and strangest) ministry opportunities in the face. Growing up I wanted to be a rock star (a life with a lot less stress and a lot more fun than that of a pastor). But all those years of playing air guitar to the Rolling Stones in front of my bedroom mirror didn't pay off. After a stint playing in a rock band in Albuquerque, New Mexico, I traded in my band equipment for college and later graduate school, where I majored in philosophy and biblical studies. Along the way came a calling to serve as a pastor. I never would have scripted the path. I mean, come on, which would you choose—being a pastor or a rock star? But I absolutely loved being a pastor. I loved meeting people and hearing their stories, seeing them come to faith, watching the difference God made in their lives as they followed Him. I enjoyed playing a small part in helping people find healing and forgiveness—and now I was headed to a place in dire need of both.

What intrigued me most about Vegas was not the non-stop gaming and entertainment. It was the sense that our family belonged in America's most notorious city, and that God belonged there too. Though I am a conservative Christian, I will do *anything* that does not violate the Bible to help people experience God's grace. I knew there would be plenty of desperate, hurting people in the Vegas area. And desperate measures would be needed to show them there is hope for everyone, no matter how broken he or she might be. I had experienced that hope in my life, and I wanted to share it with others.

The brilliant social critic Neil Postman argued that in every era there is one city that captures the American spirit and becomes its symbolic center. In the Revolutionary era, that city was Boston, with its cry for freedom. In the mid-nineteenth century, New York, a melting pot of diverse cultures, became the symbolic center. In the early twentieth century, Chicago embodied the spirit of entrepreneurial adventure with its railroads, steel mills, and cattle. "Today," Postman says, "we must look to the city of Las Vegas, Nevada, as a metaphor for our national spirit and aspiration, its symbol a thirty-foot-high cardboard picture of a slot machine and a chorus girl. For Las Vegas is a city entirely devoted to the idea of entertainment, and as such proclaims the spirit of a culture in which all public discourse increasingly takes the form of entertainment."[1]

Whether you agree or disagree with Postman, the Vegas phenomenon is critical to understanding not only where we are as a culture, but also where the rest of America is headed. Like it or not, America is looking more like Vegas every day.

Vegas is a town where anything goes, where people are accepted for who they are, where strange is normal. I mean, after a while it doesn't seem odd that your neighbor is washing his car in his driveway at 5:30 a.m. because he just got home from work. Yet it is also a town of great optimism, great faith, and a contagious openness to God. In short order, I fell in love with the town and its people, with its quirkiness, with its brokenness and pain.

Today I see Vegas as a remarkable place where God is doing remarkable things, with stories of new beginnings at almost every turn. And I've noticed that every story hinges on a mysterious gift called grace. Grace can be defined as God's extravagant favor and forgiveness toward His undeserving children—and 'undeserving' would have to include all of us. But in Vegas, where people seem to need grace most and expect it least, I witness what I call "uncensored grace." Uncensored grace is what you get from a loving God when all the religious types have gone home, and every last hope for your own effort has blown up in your face. Uncensored means that there is no formula or membership or performance that stands between you and God's goodness. Uncensored means that as wide and deep and high as your mountain of personal ruin might get, God's transforming grace is always wider and deeper and higher.

A gambler once claimed that Vegas is the only city in America where, when people pray, they really mean it. I've found that people here do mean it when they pray, but for much better reasons than a bet. Maybe you have reasons to pray as well. Perhaps the doubting and struggling of your own life will be mirrored in these pages. If so, the people you meet will show you there is something more. Their lives speak of the purpose faith can bring into your life.

The pressure of relationships, kids, and work is overwhelming. You long for something real in your faith, not pretense and clichés. Nothing frustrates you more than judgmental and self-righteous religious types. I believe the true stories in *Uncensored Grace* will bring you encouragement and inspiration by sharing with you the humility and honesty you've been searching for.

Perhaps you feel disqualified from life by your past. It could be drug addiction, an affair, a betrayal, or a dream that was never fulfilled. The sense of guilt hangs over you like a cloud. But there is good news. The people you're about to meet want you to know that there is forgiveness and hope no matter what you have done or experienced.

It has been said that "what happens in Vegas stays in Vegas." But we couldn't keep these stories to ourselves— because what happens in Vegas could change your life. When

I first visited this city, I didn't know what to expect, except the unexpected. I was not disappointed. And as we explore a fresh vision of the Christian faith and a different side of Vegas together, I guarantee you won't be disappointed either.

Skin to Skin

Donte and Stephanie's Story

I f gambling is Las Vegas's first business, sex—the showing of it, the selling of it, the glorifying in it—is the second.

Years ago, when Vegas was little more than a railroad depot for trains between Salt Lake City and Los Angeles, prostitution was legal. There were no "entertainment" services that would send a girl to your hotel room, no hustlers handing out lurid sex-show cards. The prostitutes were lodged in a boarding house near the depot and most everybody knew where it was.

Hookers were eventually outlawed (though prostitution is still legal in other counties in Nevada), but the advent of Bugsy Siegel and the mob's rule of Vegas made sure that many of them stayed off the unemployment line. Soon the building of the great casino-hotels ushered in the age of the scantily clad showgirl. Revues like "Lido de Paris"—which wouldn't have passed muster then in New York or Los Angeles—made voyeurism a civic virtue.

Las Vegas went through a flirtation with family entertainment a decade ago. But now, as *Time* magazine writes, "Vegas has reinvented itself again, returning to vice but sanitizing it by creating the biggest, nicest place to sin ever imagined, a Sodom and Gomorrah without the guilt."[2]

Some dealers at the Rio, a pleasure palace that caters to the twentysomethings, wear thong bikinis at night. And, as *Time*[3] noted, one of the Cirque du Soleil shows "is a virtually naked gymnastics event in which men make out and the rest of the cast simulates acrobatic sex." In an adult show at the MGM Grand, "the dancers' costumes consist of a stringless G-string, one of many great new technologies to come from Las Vegas." At the Palms and the Hard Rock, two hotels that attract the Hollywood set, some suites for high rollers now come equipped with in-room stripper's poles. You can see anything in Vegas.

So what would you expect to find at ten-thirty at night inside a 350-seat theater in one of the most luxurious hotels on probably the best-known boulevard in the United States? A professional adult show featuring eight women who are about to bare themselves.

Each of them is fulsome, chosen for her beauty and dancing prowess. They wear high heels and G-strings, and are outfitted in six-inch-wide rhinestone necklaces and long leather gloves. Partridge headdresses festoon their hair. They cover their chests in the opening minutes with feather boas and dance on various levels of the stage to the up-tempo beat of the music.

Eventually the score becomes slower and more sensual. One by one they discard their feathers. Soon they are fully uncovered from the navel up and are establishing eye contact with members of the audience.

The crowd of about three hundred contains more couples than single men. Compared with other adult shows on the Strip, this one's choreography makes it seem relatively tasteful. There are few hoots and hollers as the women twist and throw back their shoulders. But the show's intent is to arouse.

A burlesque-style comedienne and a tap dancer fill breaks

when the showgirls change costumes. For the remainder of the show, the girls are topless from the start on some numbers and covered on others. They all have been selected for their dancing skills, athleticism, bodies, and looks.

Before the hour-and-a-quarter show is over, the lead dancer, Stephanie Keene, sits on a chair with her back to the audience and, facing a mirror, performs a highly sensual striptease. Five feet eight inches tall off stage, five-eleven-and-a-half in her heels, she is unquestionably the star of the show. All eyes are on her.

Stephanie works one or two shows a night, six nights a week, fifty weeks a year. It is a tough business, and it usually leaves her exhausted the following morning. A huge picture of her in heels, G-string, and nothing else, taken from her left with her arms folded across her chest, has appeared in the arrival concourses at Vegas's McCarran Airport. The shot emphasizes her long legs, arms, and fingers, and her dark, flowing hair.

This picture and another of her have been spread across billboards next to Interstate 15, just west of the Strip. When she passes by them on her twenty-minute drive to work, she wishes deep down that they weren't there.

Stephanie Keene is a Bible-reading, 10-percent-tithing church attendee who has been baptized by immersion and given her heart to Jesus Christ.

Several blocks down the Strip at another well-known casino, a second adult show has just begun. Unlike the first, it is designed to appeal to women as well as to men. Besides five women in various stages of undress, this production features three male dancers who wear black leather jackets that expose their chests.

Some of the women are as beautiful as those in Stephanie's show. They are outfitted at the start in nothing more than G-strings, straps that form an X in front, and exotic Egyptian-like headdresses. All of them are professional, Broadway-quality dancers, and for awhile each performs in an illusionary style, with one arm held horizontally to shield her breasts from view.

Shortly after the men take part in the dance, the women uncover themselves. The theater crowd of three hundred sits grandstand style, almost on top of the stage. The men, who resemble ballet dancers in their movements, have sculpted bodies that glisten under the lighting. The lead male dancer, Donte Harrison, serves as the show's emcee and sole singer. He has marvelous range and vocal gifts, but it is his slow striptease in the midst of the uncovered women that is the cabaret-style show's centerpiece.

Donte's show pushes the envelope more than Stephanie's. Most of the music is heavy metal. There's more skin-against-skin contact and quite a bit of sensual touching. The lights are red and the stage is frequently mirrored. As the women dance around him, Donte removes his black top hat, cape, and pants until he wears just a pair of thong briefs. Every ripple of his six-feet-two-inch body shines in the spotlight in the midst of the women.

As he says at the start of the show, "This is Las Vegas! It's all right to get a little rowdy."

Donte Harrison is Stephanie Keene's husband.

He too has given his heart to Christ. He reads the Bible daily and attends church with Stephanie each weekend. It was he who first pushed to raise their tithe to 10 percent.

What is a Las Vegas showgirl like?

Not necessarily what you'd think.

Stephanie, thirty-five, is sweet, gentle, and transparent. She is shy and retiring around strangers until she gets to know them. If you passed her in her usual jeans and loose-fitting turtleneck in a Vegas supermarket, you would consider her attractive but probably not imagine her profession.

Her path to the Vegas world began at age two and a half. A native of Canada, she had a grandmother who owned a dance studio. She was a natural from the get-go and essentially grew up there. After getting a college degree in theater arts, she sailed the world for cruise lines, appearing in pocket-size musical revues based on Broadway or movie themes.

She had taken dance lessons since childhood, so she shot to the lead of most of the shows she was in. The contracts she signed were not lavish—$500 to $1,000 a week. But there was no overhead. She had free room and board on ship, staying in a small private cabin. And the sightseeing, of course, was gratis.

It was a well-ordered life, and Stephanie had her priorities. She herself headed the list. Then came dancing, getting the next job…traveling to new countries, making money… having fun, going out, meeting friends. It amounted to a fairly common, early-twenties feel-good chart. Family was vaguely in the mix, but not within the top five. God, a nebulous concept, wasn't even on the list.

If God was off her chart, however, Stephanie certainly happened to be on His.

Her path to faith began bumpily.

When she was a senior in college, her mother was hospitalized with endocarditis, an inflammation of the heart membrane that began to attack other vital organs. Jane Keene was desperately ill. And in the vortex of that illness, she turned her life over to God completely and irretrievably.

Amazingly, she soon recovered. And with the evidence of

her healing she became fervent in her faith almost overnight, zealously spreading the word and urging Stephanie and her two brothers to believe. While still in the hospital, in fact, Jane prevailed on Stephanie to pray and be saved right in front of her.

"I didn't really understand it, and I wasn't that serious about it for myself," Stephanie recalls. "But I did go ahead and pray the prayer."

In reality, the whole idea seemed to be nonsense. "Our family was like, 'Okay, Jane, relax a little bit!'" Stephanie says. "It was just kind of weird."

For the rest of her twenties, Stephanie could not have cared less about God.

After finishing one of her cruise contracts, she came to Vegas with a boyfriend to check out its show scene. Though there were still plenty of entry-level gigs around, she found there were fewer and fewer dance spots available that paid enough for someone to make a living. Except, that is, in adult entertainment.

One evening her boyfriend suggested they see an adult show downtown at the Plaza Hotel.

"I was like, 'Yeah, okay, let's go look,' although I'd told him I was *never* going to do a topless show. I felt it was too degrading.

"When I saw it, I was taken aback at first by the topless thing. Then I began to think, *Hmm, it's risqué, but it's still fairly tasteful.* The girls were uncovered, but they were dancers, not strippers."

Before the month was out, she wound up auditioning for Nicholas Griffin Productions. Griffin was a former cruise-line producer who had recently begun to stage musical revues as well as topless shows in Tahoe, Reno, and Tokyo. He immediately saw Stephanie's talent and offered her a prime role in the Tokyo show. Although she had never dreamed of being in an adult production, she signed up for three months.

"I never told my parents what kind of a show it was. And for me it was uncomfortable the first two or three nights. But then after a few shows, I'm dancing, I'm doing difficult, challenging choreography, the production was of high quality, and the topless thing just kind of faded into the background."

Returning to the States, she spent a few more years in cruise-ship work. But soon she was back in Nevada, working the Laughlin, Reno, and Lake Tahoe circuit for none other than Griffin.

He was quickly changing the way show business worked in Nevada, locking up a small group of players and having them perform both a family revue and an adult show each night. It was a two-for-one deal that kept down both his costs and those of the hotel-casinos. But for many of the dancers, it meant edging into adult work or risking unemployment.

The troupe performed in the family show each night at seven-thirty—usually a revue such as "New York, New York"—and then a topless show, "Skin to Skin," at ten-thirty. Stephanie was soon the best at what she did and was making two to three times what a school teacher brought home.

For all of her success, though, Stephanie was headed for her first heartbreak.

She had hooked up romantically with a singer and dancer in the company. Within a few months they were married. Almost immediately afterward she developed a vague uneasiness—a sense that Brian was being unfaithful to her.

Brian finally confessed that he'd been cheating—and the infidelity was with one of her friends, no less. Stephanie tried to stick it out, but marriage therapy didn't work. She and Brian were divorced in a year and a half. Like tens of thousands of others from Vegas to Reno, she was far from her family, broken, and feeling totally alone.

She filled the void with constant dating, which led to several new relationships. All were short and painful. "I guess I believed in God more than I thought because I'd sometimes ask Him, *Why am I in this mess?*" she recalls. "*Why on earth are You putting me through this?*"

A few months later, a lead "New York, New York" cast member took sick and Griffin had to quickly find a substitute. He had a player in his identical revue in Atlantic City fly in to Reno and fill the part.

The new guy was Donte. He says, "As soon as I saw Stephanie, I was taken and she was taken. I remember thinking, *Whew, it's good I'm here only for one performance because I'd better not look at her ever again!*"

Donte Harrison is confident, open, and extremely articulate—the Bryant Gumbel, if you will, of the Vegas adult-show world. He can not only dance with Broadway ability but also sing and hold a show together with the microphone at the same time.

He was a military brat, the son of an army lieutenant who rose to become a colonel at the Pentagon. He grew up on an endless succession of military bases—Fort Benning, Georgia; Fort Leavenworth, Kansas; Fort Bragg, North Carolina; and others. He was always the new kid on the block, settling down only when he got to high school.

Donte was a born singer, an obvious talent by age four. Attending James Madison University in Virginia, he wanted to major in theater arts and begin a singing career. His dad nixed the idea, so Donte got a bachelor's in broadcast communication.

Donte's father, the son of a preacher and a deacon, commanded that all five members of the family attend church on the military base every Sunday. But in reality they all practiced religion by rote. Not until his folks' faith came alive in their late forties did God even climb within Donte's frame of reference.

"I use the totem pole analogy because it's so relevant to my life," he says. "I believed there was a God, and I knew there was a Jesus, but faith was so low on the pole it wasn't even close to a priority.

"I was first, then my career, then singing or auditioning for something, then a girl. Family was kind of in there, but faith was not even close. Kind of pathetic when I look back on it."

Like Stephanie, Donte went straight into cruise-line productions after college. The average showbiz career on cruise ships is five years. Perhaps because of his ability—he was always the star—he put in upwards of ten.

From time to time Donte's mom sent him Christian tapes or books, similar to those Stephanie's mother was mailing to her. He wasn't interested in religion or preachers. He had seen the scandals that brought TV evangelists down. He had become hardened, even hostile, to anything dealing with faith.

Donte eventually saw a couple of Griffin's topless shows in Nevada. He signed on as the lead singer of one of the productions that shifted between Tahoe and Reno. The music was high-energy rock, pop, and rhythm and blues. The content, from the dancing to the comedian's humor, was, for him, highly sexual.

"You just rationalize that it's really okay," he says. "I'm not saying it was so okay that I told my parents about it right away. At first it was sensual and arousing, and it was a challenge to get used to it. But once you cross over the bridge and get a little detached, it's just a gig. After a month or two it becomes routine."

One night a pal of Donte's brought two women to the

show. Just for fun, the friend asked him to bring one of the women up for a cameo on stage—dressed, of course. Her name was Candace, and Donte was struck by the cocktail waitress and schoolteacher. At thirty-one, after a decade on stage, he found it liberating to be with someone from outside the business.

Soon the two of them were married.

Candace thought they would get a house with a white picket fence while Donte found a nine-to-five job. Donte assumed he would stay on the stage. They married blind—"like changing costumes in a show," he says. It was over in a few months, and when he got the divorce papers, it was the lowest point in his life.

Within months he got involved with another woman from outside the business. He and Keena were talking about having children. He was not going to make the same mistakes with her that he had with Candace. He would leave dancing. He had already picked out their wedding rings.

But a few months in, he felt deader than ever and walked away from the relationship.

He was tumbling now, running up big-time debt. He wanted a wardrobe that befitted his position as a lead performer, so he put it on his card. He charged a home studio in which he could record new songs. He bought a new, fast car on credit every six to nine months.

"You can get upside down in debt in a hurry that way," Donte says. "After the divorce I was just a mess. I'm the lead, and I'm making money, and I'm getting all this applause, yet I'm empty. My mom was sending me Christian tapes and a devotional magazine, and I started saying to myself, 'Lord, what am I doing? This can't be what You have in mind.'"

Today, Donte considers the low points of his broken marriage and follow-up relationship the moments God first began to work in his heart.

He also thinks it was more than coincidence that Stephanie, whom he had met the previous year, was now appearing with him twice a night in Reno, in the family show at seven-thirty and the topless one at ten. They had been taken with each other at first. They had watched each other from a distance as they each went through divorce. And now they were simply becoming friends.

In reaction to declining revenues at the gaming tables in the 1990s, Las Vegas tried to make the Strip a family affair. Circus Circus built a mammoth enclosed arcade. New York-New York opened with a roller coaster. There were pirate battles every thirty minutes at Treasure Island.

But by the end of the decade it was out with the kids, in with the showgirls.

Denise Jones Productions lured Stephanie to Vegas for the adult show she would make famous—one reviewer likened it to "Playboy meets MTV." Two years later Griffin brought Donte to town for the show that pushed the envelope a little further.

Friends in Reno, Donte and Stephanie were at first strangers in Vegas.

"We had been dating other people in town for awhile and had kind of lost touch," Stephanie remembers. "Finally I e-mailed him and said, 'Sorry, I've been a little out of it. I've been going through a lot. I had another relationship break up on me.'

"He e-mailed me back. We each knew about the other's marriage that went bad, but neither of us had known about the second relationships we both had that didn't work out."

Donte recalls, "We had a lot to talk about."

The e-mails led to phone calls. There were talks about how they tried to will their latest situations to work, but they both felt empty one month into them. One night Donte came over to see Stephanie's show, and afterward they went to the Shadow Bar at Caesars. They each had a drink. They had had drinks before, but this time it seemed different.

They talked about their emotional deadness. It was a strange topic for them.

Finally, Donte heard himself saying, "Steph, you know what? I really want to start going to a church, but I don't know where to find one."

While in Reno, Stephanie had visited a nondenominational church for two years. She found it in the phone book and had begun attending during her marriage, when she realized her life was short of something. Whenever she went, it gave her a sense of meaning and belonging. But she needed someone to discuss her feelings with, since faith was increasingly stirring her interest.

"Oh, I go to a church sometimes," Stephanie said. "I was thinking of going tomorrow."

"You mind if I go with you?" Donte asked.

And so their second date happened to be at Central. It was roughly at the lowest point in Donte's life.

"It came at a time when I had finally started listening to the tapes my mother had been sending me for years," he says. "I felt I was such a disappointment to everybody. I was ashamed, I felt guilty, I was upset, I didn't know what to do or where to go."

It was an unusual service. At the end of his message, Pastor Jud told the congregation to bow their heads and close their eyes. Then he said that if any people wanted to have a relationship with God, the first step was to raise their hands, and he would pray for them.

"My hand shot up immediately," Donte recalls.

He now realizes it was the moment he connected with God. He had literally reached out. It was also his first real date with Stephanie, the moment they began growing beyond mere friendship. Instead of going to the Shadow Bar for brunch, they went to Blueberry Hill, a pancake house in suburban Henderson.

To use Donte's totem pole analogy, God had just jumped from the bottom to very near the top for both of them. But they had no one at their jobs to talk with about God—at least they didn't think so at the time. And they had a gorilla of a question hanging over them: They performed in topless shows…how was *this* going to work?

Stephanie and Donte decided to take what was happening one step at a time and to put that question aside for the moment.

They enrolled in a two-month class at Central to learn the basics of the Christian faith. Then they decided to get baptized— in a pool in loose-fitting clothes in front of bright lights and before hundreds of onlookers. Stephanie can't pinpoint the moment she first believed, but she knows Jesus was in her heart by the time she was dipped into the water.

Two friends were suddenly seeing each other through entirely different eyes.

Stephanie had found her spiritual center and had someone to share it with.

Donte had found not just faith but another gift—as he says, the gentlest and sweetest woman in the world.

They fell head over heels in love.

Stephanie and Donte were married in 2003. They bought a home on a cul-de-sac in the Vegas suburbs. Just your everyday couple. Two adult dancers in a one-level ranch house with a pool and spa out back, a gym in the garage, a golden retriever for company, two red SUVs in the driveway, and a very strict budget to retire their debt.

They plan to start a family soon. At their ages, they can see the day coming when they won't be the top dancers on the Strip. Stephanie hopes to find a part-time job and become a mom. Donte plans to be a dad and a TV journalist. They have embarked on a lifetime adventure together.

When Stephanie's final curtain falls, it will be both sad and something of a relief to her. The truth is that Stephanie's job, as well as Donte's, has increasingly represented a conflict for her since they became believers and started growing in their faith.

Make no mistake, she still relishes what she does. She views herself as a dancer, not a sex object, and she is not playing in Hoboken. She is one of about ten principal dancers on the Strip and perhaps the most critically acclaimed. The athleticism, the lights, the split-second timing of the routines, the electricity backstage just before the show starts—all produce highs for her.

"But the conflict is still there," she says. "I experience it with my faith every night to some extent. Some nights it's not bad. Some nights it's really, really strong.

"The fact is, I'm dancing topless. I'm performing for other people in a sensual and sexual manner. I can see the audience, and I try to focus on the couples who are smiling and enjoying themselves. But I'm still performing for people out there who are thinking lustful things."

Donte, who has emceed telethons and hopes to segue into

a career as a TV entertainment reporter, says, "I'm ready yesterday" to change careers.

"When you feel embarrassed about what you do, that's a conflict," he says. "I'd love to sing at church, and Steph would love to become part of the arts ministry there, but neither of us would feel comfortable doing that if we've been in a topless show the night before."

But who would have thought the premier adult dancers in Sin City would turn out to be believers? Donte and Stephanie now believe God brought them together in these shows for a reason.

What have they learned from their remarkable journey?

That He met them where they were.

And that He holds their future.

The Shoes of a Fisherman

Sonny's Story

I n the ancient world it used to be said that all roads lead to Rome.

In today's world, at least in the America of broken relationships, it might be said that all roads lead to Vegas.

It's a place where you can be anonymous. Where you can disassociate yourself from your past. Where you can start over. Where you can be exactly who you are, even with all your warts and hang-ups.

Hundreds of singles arrive in Vegas each day, coming by plane to McCarran Airport, arriving by bus at the Greyhound depot, cruising in on I-15 or Route 95 in a new car they'll never pay off or a clunker that will be towed away tomorrow.

And what do they do? Where do they go?

When Sonny McKenna arrived in Vegas, running from his misbegotten past in California, he went straight to Binion's Horseshoe, the famous old bar and casino on Fremont Street. He was weary and trying to get away from his heroin habit.

Early tomorrow morning, he told himself, he would take his gear from the trunk of his car and go out bass fishing on Lake Mead. He had heard about the fishing but had never been there. He was an expert with a rod and reel—it was his one success in life other than selling drugs for profit.

But tonight he just wanted to sit at the bar, have a beer, and survey the territory. He was nursing a Bud when a guy came up, looking in both directions, asking what he was doing in town.

Sonny told him he was fleeing San Diego, trying to kick his habit. The conversation got around to Sonny's valuable El Camino, a car he had built from the ground up.

"Well, c'mon dude, let's go get loaded," the guy said. They went off, the guy invited some friends over, and they all got high. Party time, first night in town. And the "friends" would not only share their smack. They were also willing to teach Sonny how to make some serious money.

It turned out they were members of a counterfeiting ring that worked the bars, the 7-Elevens, and a number of the casinos. They made their own coins and used them in the slot machines. It was beautiful—the slots took the phony coins and the gang took the winnings.

In fifteen years Sonny would be arrested in Vegas twelve times. He would be booked for everything from making his own silver dollars to soliciting a prostitute to possession of ten bags of heroin to carrying narcotics paraphernalia to vagrancy to trespassing. At one point he became one of the most wanted men in Nevada. Even the FBI was after him.

Sonny McKenna, a moth attracted by the Vegas lights.

Sonny McKenna, scam artist.

In only one respect was Sonny's childhood peaceful.

It was early in the morning, an hour after dawn. All was stillness on the pond.

"This is the spot, Sonny," his stepfather said. "We'll stop right here."

He didn't say another word, but pulled the oars from the water and placed them silently and carefully in the bow. Sonny watched intently now as the man he called his father took a small, bright red Rebel lure and attached it to the end of the six-year-old's line.

Sonny took the rod in his small hands. He cast the line and lure out onto the water's surface, as he had often seen his father do. No one uttered a word now. The first rays of sunlight made their way through the trees and reached the surface of the water.

Ever so slowly Sonny began drawing the lure back to the boat. It was creeping across the water now, the eyes of both Sonny and his father fixed upon it. Suddenly, a glint beneath the surface! And a split second later the plane of the water exploded as a four-pound bass, its mouth wide open, its eyes fierce and straining, struck at the lure.

Sonny pulled on the line a moment too soon and the bass missed. But oh, the excitement of it! The power and glory of the encounter! From that moment on, the boy was a bass fisherman.

But off the pond, all was not so calm.

Sonny was the son of a twelve-and-a-half-year-old mother and a father who deserted her. He grew up in a home where his mother, a bank teller, and his stepfather, a used-car salesman, were often drunk and abusive, sometimes beating Sonny with a belt from his neck to his knees, until bloodied.

Desperate for acceptance, Sonny began to find it in all the wrong places. He started smoking pot, running away, always in and out of detention centers, returning to drugs and trouble whenever he got out. Eventually he became so uncontrollable his folks just let him go. He went to San Francisco to live with hippie friends who would foster his drug habit.

The spiral continued—and worsened.

He quickly got into the drug trade, selling one-ounce portions of pot. A few rock stars started buying from him, giving his business a certain cachet. And soon he was making enough to do all his own drugs and buy his first Harley-Davidson besides.

After a few years, Sonny hooked up with a girl from his hometown he had known when they were ten. She was unlike the people he lived with. She wasn't into drugs and the rock scene—unlike him she was straight.

Within a few months she was pregnant with his child. Gradually she prevailed on him to leave San Francisco, ditch the drug culture, and move to Los Angeles. Surprising even himself, Sonny agreed. They moved to the City of Angels, renting a small apartment. And he stacked groceries in a supermarket at less than $100 a week.

But a new city didn't change Sonny. His addiction followed him to LA, along with his selfishness, his restlessness, and the scars from his past.

Sonny's wife left with her head down but eventually remarried. Their son turned out to be the wealthy CEO of a power company. As of this writing, Sonny has never met him. For all Sonny knows, he may have other sons and daughters. They just weren't priorities then.

Alone now in LA, Sonny asked himself why he should be working in the stupid supermarket when he could be selling drugs again. LA at the time was the hot spot for rockers, so he had no problem moving his drugs. He made $75,000 to $100,000 a year—the equivalent of $375,000 to $500,000 today. He was driving a huge Harley and a pristine Pontiac Bonneville.

"The more I made, the more I spent," he says. "It was just

live good today and never mind tomorrow."

And besides, Sonny always had his fishing.

Even through the drug times, between the staggered prison terms, between the bouts with heroin and crack cocaine, the fishing was always his escape, his commune with nature.

It brought him back to the Rebel lure floating silently on the water.

Sonny was twenty-three. He was at a big party in Monterey, feeling like an operator. He walked into the bathroom on a high, only to find a friend and another guy there fixing heroin.

"You want some?" they asked.

"Why not?" he said.

It was all so casual and incidental. He had always wondered what it would be like, and here was his chance.

He rolled up his sleeve, tied his arm so the vein stood out, and injected himself. Up to that point, the strongest drug he had tried was cocaine. He didn't really care for that. It made him hyper and paranoid.

Now, with the heroin surge, it was as if his body were saying, *Sonny, this doesn't belong here.* He immediately began throwing up and couldn't stop. Then he fell asleep, woke up, and threw up again, repeating the cycle until the drug was out of his system. It was horrendous.

And guess what? He used heroin again the following week and found it better. He didn't throw up as much. The highs seemed longer and quite wonderful. No matter what worries he had, the heroin made him not care.

"The first time I took it I was a heroin addict all ready to go," he says.

Sonny soon moved to Monterey to be closer to his suppliers. And as soon as he got there his heroin habit worsened. It went from once a week to twice to three times a week. Then every day to three times a day to eight times a day. Within six months he could hardly get out of bed without shooting up.

"When you first start using heroin, you're unconscious," he says. "But the more addicted you become, the more you can cope. Pretty soon you're always jittery and it takes the heroin to make you normal. After awhile you have to have it just to eat.

"Then three hours go by, and little by little you start getting jittery, and your stomach gets upset—time for more."

And the addiction costs big bucks—more than $1,000 a day in Sonny's case, or more than his drug sales could support. Even selling guns from his extensive $40,000 collection only bought him a few more hits.

It got to the point where he would roam neighborhoods in his panel truck, break into houses, and steal every valuable he found. Eventually, he was arrested and convicted after having stolen forty-five color television sets from a Holiday Inn. His sentence was another year in prison, this time in the Monterey County Jail. And three decades later, his memory of that first month there remains stark and vivid.

When you're imprisoned with a habit like Sonny's, there's no methadone, no soft cushion. He slept hardly at all for an entire month. He sweated so hard that he soaked his bed sheets, the padding, and the mattress as well. He lost thirty pounds. He had diarrhea and threw up at the same time. Anything he put in his stomach he heaved.

People don't break heroin habits by themselves. It's a monster no one wants to meet. It takes control of your mind and body. No man's will is strong enough to break it. The only ways are methadone and cold turkey—and in the Monterey jail it was cold turkey.

It was like being in hell. In that first month, the heroin got in Sonny's very bones. He felt like he was 120 years old. He ached from the inside out. Every time he moved his arms or legs he felt they were going to break.

But he did get off the heroin. He did it the jail's way.

As for God, Sonny was on the other side of the desert. He didn't believe there was a God. Look at his life—how could there be? If somebody had asked him, he probably would have said he believed in evil more than God. Drugs were his Jesus. If there was a God, it was Jimi Hendrix.

The day Sonny got out of jail, it took him two hours before he had another needle in his arm.

Years passed, and Sonny embarked on what he hoped would be a new direction in his life. He moved to San Diego and enrolled in a nursing school. Now he was able to break his habit for stretches, sometimes staying off drugs long enough to live a fairly normal life.

Older now, he got his nursing license and formed a series of longer relationships with women, sometimes lasting a year or two. And, never forgetting that one perfect day when the bass broke the surface of the pond and went for the lure, he turned to fishing.

At one point he was living with a woman exasperated by his fishing habits—he would leave home at dawn, fish on a lake all day, and return at dusk. She gave him an ultimatum. Either enter some of the professional bass-fishing tournaments so popular around San Diego, or move on.

Sonny won the first tournament he entered. And from that

point on, whenever drug free, he dedicated himself to making the pro bass ranks. He won a number of local tournaments, earning $1,000 here and a few thousand there. He traveled the country fishing in the lucrative U.S. Open championships.

Before long, it was as if he were leading two lives. He was a repeated drug user with a prison record in one incarnation. And, in the other, he was an increasingly well-known prize fisherman who was featured once on an ESPN bass-fishing show.

Sonny found himself staying off drugs for longer stretches, but the heroin still stalked him, eventually pushing him to rob another house. But someone had seen him climbing in the window, and the cops were waiting when he walked outside.

He spent another year in jail. And after his release, he headed for Vegas.

Vegas was always a wide-open place for Sonny, a town where he could do some hustling, buy his drugs, go straight as a nurse for awhile, fit in the cracks.

After spending another year in the slammer for the counterfeiting scam, Sonny soon found himself at Binion's Horseshoe drinking another beer. He had been clean for awhile, but feeling depressed and listless, it didn't take him long to find a woman who could get him the drugs he needed.

And within an hour he was shooting up in his weekly rented room at a dingy motel. The following day he intentionally overdosed—he wanted to end his life—only to fall into a deep sleep instead.

A few hours later he awoke in a stupor, got up, and went to the bathroom. He was so groggy standing there that he lost his balance and fell against a wall, freakishly breaking the two large bones in his lower leg, with one of them sticking through the skin.

Sonny managed to get himself to the door of the hotel room, but he barely had enough strength to open the door. Luckily, a homeless man walked by as he was lying on the floor in the doorway. Sonny told him to flush the drugs down the toilet so the authorities wouldn't discover them when the ambulance arrived.

It was, in a sense, the best day of his life.

He was taken to University Medical Center, placed on methadone and kept for a month. And when he was discharged, he was assigned as a live-in nurse to a widow nearing eighty. As he soon realized, he was the son she never had. And she was the mother and grandmother he never knew.

Her name was Mimi. She was the first person he ever loved.

She lived in a sizable home near Tropicana. Sonny's job was to hobble around in his full-legged cast, cook for her, clean house, and keep track of her doctors' appointments. Mimi's job was to believe in him. Whenever he wanted to do something like go fishing or buy a new motorcycle, she'd take a big breath, smile, and say, "You go, Sonny!"

Their affection was pure and full of grace.

He told her about his life, and she may have seen something redeemable in him—Mimi's daughter was a gambling addict who had rarely visited her. He told her he was a drug addict trying to get clean, and she said, "Thanks for being honest, Sonny. Now you keep it up!"

An invalid, she was too much a lady to allow him to wash her. Only when he convinced her that this was his job and that she had gone two months without a shower did she relent. She was a believer who watched Christian speakers on television with him on Sundays. It was the first time Sonny had ever listened to the message.

Sonny had an old bass-fishing boat that he used to take out on weekends to Lakes Mead, Havasu, and Mohave farther south. It got to the point where he was winning most every tournament he entered, becoming one of the best-known fishermen in the West.

In a sense, fishing was his circle of calm within the fire. Drugs were the farthest thing from his mind when he had a rod and reel in hand.

"You have to have an instinct to fish with the pros, and I have that instinct," Sonny says. "I can tell you when a fish breathes on my bait."

He had placed in a couple of national tournaments—the big babies where you can win $1 million—and was saving $45,000 to buy a new boat for the U.S. Open.

"Sonny, how much have you saved for your boat?" Mimi asked one day.

"Twenty-two thousand dollars," he replied.

"Let's go get your boat," she said. "I've got the rest."

She paid him $750 and then $1,000 a week. He was with her for seven years, and every night until her final-year slide into dementia she prayed for him. More than anything, he was confused by her praying. He knew there was an alcoholic, drug-addicted, kick-you-on-your-butt sick man inside himself, and he knew nothing about asking God for forgiveness.

And then came Mimi's descent.

She broke her hip at home and had replacement surgery. And gradually she lost her mind. She thought she was home in Los Angeles. She started talking to her late husband. It fell to Sonny to remind her she was actually in Vegas.

Mimi died during the Christmas season, a year after

Sonny had started using drugs again. He had made remarkable strides. He owned a new bass boat, a NASCAR F-150 Ford truck, and a motor home, all fully paid for. And he had more than $250,000 in the bank. But he was smoking one ounce a day of a miracle drug he had just discovered—crack cocaine. Soon he had a habit of $1,000 a day.

Sonny had been using since Mimi started losing her mind. Crack is an upper that makes you feel happier. And now that she was gone he went off the deep end. He smoked every dollar in his savings account, along with his boat, his truck, his new cycle, his motor home, even his leather jackets and Harley shirts. He was a walking man now. He'd walk to a hotel on Boulder Highway and buy as much crack as he could. He didn't sleep or eat. He neglected everything. The upkeep on Mimi's house? The bills for the utilities and the cable? *Give me the crack.*

Go ahead, he thought, *give me an eviction notice.*

And a year later the authorities complied. They threw him out of Mimi's house. He put some jeans and T-shirts in a backpack and hit the streets. It was his final odyssey.

For eight months Sonny was homeless. Through the winter and into the spring, huddling under dirty quilts and blankets. Bedding down in the tall grass behind a Department of Motor Vehicles office. Never bathing, never showering, using the bathrooms at the hamburger chains, never washing his clothes.

There is a skill to being homeless—a way of hiding in the cracks and staying under the radar. But Sonny at first had yet to master it. He was desperate for drugs and could spot a dealer from fifty yards off. He had found his place in the

...t he literally had no money. And he didn't know the

...day he saw a homeless guy with a spray bottle who was washing the windows on cars as they pulled into a shopping center. So he became a windshield man. "Sir" or "Ma'am," he'd say, "can I clean the windows on your car?" Nine times out of ten they would give him a buck or two even if they didn't want him touching it.

He looked terrible. His weight was 160 and falling fast, his hair was matted and unkempt, his mouth was a slash in the midst of his beard. And on top of that you could smell him from ten feet away. It got to the point where some of the homeless—those who had been living in the lot long enough to learn where to shower—would steer clear of him.

Once in awhile he would wash a window and the driver would hand him $20. They'd ask him how he got there. He told them the truth, that he was an addict. Then he'd take the $20 and spend it on crack.

Once he was working a bank lot on Charleston. A woman walked out, and he asked if he could do her windows. Instead of saying yes, she asked if she could hold his hands. It was okay by him, a little weird maybe, but she started praying, calling down the Holy Spirit, asking for the demons to leave.

"That was pretty cool," Sonny remembers, "but it didn't make me want to change my life."

Sometimes people would simply ask if they could pray with him.

"I would say, 'You know what? If you work for this loving God, why am I in this parking lot?' I wouldn't take responsibility for what I did. My attitude was, *You take your God and your Jesus and get out of my face. You're talking to a homeless man. If your God is so loving and powerful, how come I have nowhere to live?*"

After three months in the wind and the winter rain, he got the drift of being homeless. He had the routine down. Do windows, ride the bus cross town to West Las Vegas, buy a $20 rock, ride back, smoke the cocaine in the weeds, then repeat the cycle. He would do that continually for three days, then lay down in the lot and sleep for twenty-four hours.

He went the eight months making $100 to $150 a day on the windows, and he would spend it all on crack. He would take his last hit for the night, then be unable to sleep. He told himself he would stop tomorrow, but tomorrow never came.

You would think he might have saved some money to buy a room, but it all went for crack. And twenty minutes after he smoked it, he wanted more. He ate out of garbage cans. He became adept at going behind pizza restaurants, opening boxes in the trash bins, and eating the scraps people had left.

These were the days when you drove down Fremont Street and saw nothing but crackheads. If you were out there and you were available, somebody might get you high. The only time he would sleep at either of the two downtown missions—St. Vincent's and the Las Vegas Rescue Mission—was when it rained. He couldn't put up with the missions because you couldn't smoke crack there.

At the end of his homeless cycle he weighed 130 pounds. He found some jeans, but they fell down because he didn't have a belt. When he took off his shirt in the heat of the summer, you could count his ribs.

Sometimes a simple kindness can melt the hardest heart.

Toward the summer of 2004 Sonny and some of his friends heard that Central Christian Church was offering showers and clean clothes for the homeless. Early on a Sunday morning he went there. He was eating a donut before heading downstairs to the shower room when a volunteer named Michelle approached and said, "Sir, you look like you need a hug."

He responded, "You don't want to come near me because I need a shower."

She merely put out her arms, hugged him, looked him straight in the eyes and said, "Jesus *loves* you."

That gesture and those three words began melting the ice around Sonny McKenna's heart. He had not felt love or even a human touch in weeks. He was one tough guy, but the gesture left him—what was the way to put it?—*disarmed.*

There was something different in the way she dealt with him. After the shower a short Bible study was conducted for the homeless, and for the first time he listened to what was being said.

For the next two weeks he attended services, sat in the back of Bible classes, and helped out at Central. Something was different. Though he had recently heard of people dedicating their hearts to God, he certainly hadn't handed over his. But he did have to admit he was somewhat intrigued.

Early one evening back in the field he got on his knees as the sun was beginning to set in the big Nevada sky.

The night before he had lain in the same field feeling like a loser, telling himself he didn't have a job or a home, convincing himself he would never get back on his feet, pointing out to himself that he needed to find a doctor. Fat chance of that happening.

But now he bowed down and actually put his head in the dirt. And he offered the first prayer of his life, saying beneath his breath, "Lord, You know what? I've been driving my car my whole life and all I've been doing is getting into wrecks.

From this day on I want You to drive my car."

That would have been enough to start a relationship, but he went on.

"You know, I've been learning about this Jesus. I want this Jesus to come into my heart. And I want to know more about You, God. I've denied You my whole life, but now I want to truly know You."

For the eight months he was homeless, Sonny McKenna believes he never once smiled. He had little if any interaction with people, other than the homeless. His whole conversation with the larger world amounted to "Sir... Ma'am, can I wash your windows?... Have a nice day."

He would do the windows, go get his drugs, and hide in the weeds.

But from the moment he got on his knees there was a change he has never been able to fully explain. His circumstances didn't change immediately, but he was genuinely content for the first time in his life. Before, the only peace he ever felt was in his fishing boat. But now he knew peace at an entirely different level.

"Sonny, why are you so happy all the time?" one of the guys in the weeds asked.

"Because, dude, I've found Jesus."

"What's that you're reading?"

"The Bible," Sonny said, showing him a pocket version he had picked up at church.

"Okay, now I've seen everything!"

"Hey, you guys, check this out," he'd say as he paged through the Bible. It got to the point where he was holding mini Bible studies in the field. He didn't yet have much of a grasp of what he was talking about, but he was definitely not bashful.

As for the drugs, Sonny went to God and again did most of the talking.

"God, I don't want to be doing this stuff," he said. "Would You take them over? Now here's my life. And whatever door You open, I will take that as a sign. Even if You want me to be homeless, I'll stay right here and be happy for it."

But on that night homeless friends came at him with drugs like never before. They brought pipes full of crack. He was not going to get off easily.

"Sonny, here," they said. "You're hot! You're hot! Take a hit, man!"

"Dude, I quit!" he said.

For weeks thereafter, Sonny's yearning for drugs was gone.

Soon Sonny was baptized by immersion with a group of thirty other new Christians. He did have one nightlong slipup with crack about a month later. But after all the crime, drugs, and sex, he threw himself into the church. He took part in the homeless ministry, men's groups, Bible studies, and other classes. He came on Sunday, helping organize trips to the shower for the homeless. People bought him lunches.

Impressed by his zeal, a Central member who owned a gravel and rock grinding business offered Sonny a job and a free place to stay. It was a brutal summer, and he was almost fifty-two. He was hired for the most menial of jobs—a grounds custodian. It meant that most of the time he just shoveled out the stones that fell off a conveyor belt at a gravel-grinding site south of the city.

He worked from dawn to midafternoon and was alone in a small trailer the rest of the time. No car, no contact. Just a TV, his Bible, and a woman about his age from the homeless ministry who drove out once a week to help him buy food and bring him to Central.

It was heaven to him. He spent months watching famo
Christian speakers on TV, taking notes on what they said, and
poring over the Bible. The stone-shoveling job helped give
him his dignity back. He took the Scriptures to the conveyor
belt and read them on the job.

In time, Sonny ministered to the ever-changing assort-
ment of homeless men and women he once knew. Working
with the woman who came out to the quarry, he discovered
that she sometimes had given him McDonald's meal certifi-
cates when he was homeless and washing windows.

Her name was Heather Ralston. They got to be friends.
They became dinner companions and started attending the
same Bible classes. She was his wheels. He paid for the gas,
and she did the driving. People at the church thought they
must be married because they were both in their fifties and
always together.

One day the two of them were riding in her car. He turned
toward her and, for the first time, she somehow looked different.
He had always considered her a friend, nothing more. Out at the
gravel yard he had prayed, "God, I know You have the perfect
woman for me. After all, You've said that anyone who delights
himself in the Lord, You will give him the desires of his heart…"

And now, all of a sudden…

She was driving and they happened to be talking. He
looked at her and it was kismet.

Sonny didn't say a word for a couple of weeks. First, he
prayed. Eventually he spoke to her ever so tentatively.

"You know," he said, "I've been meaning to tell you some-
thing. I can't explain this, but my feelings about you are
starting to change."

"Funny that you mention that," Heather replied. "I was
going to talk to you about my feelings too."

• • •

It's seven-thirty on a Saturday morning. All is quiet at Central.

At the end of a long hallway a handful of people move a couple of big folding tables together and gather some food-stuffs from a nearby pantry. Shafts of sunlight stream through nearby windows. A little assembly line operation begins to form.

Sonny and his wife, Heather, greet newcomers and explain the dance:

Ham and cheese between slices of bread...slip into see-through bag...packet of mustard, packet of mayo...don't forget the Scripture booklet...napkin in brown bag, insert contents...place lunches in box, each with chips, three hundred max...carry to cars... Destination: Salvation Army homeless mission.

Downtown, a line of men and women streams through the gate of a cyclone fence. They each receive a lunch bag, cup-cakes, and coffee or soda, and circle back onto the streets. All of them look older than their years. Many of them profess to be believers. They are real people, united in their plight by the unspoken knowledge of having made terrible choices.

Who would have thought Sonny would find a field of grace in Vegas?

Afterward, he points out the place where, less than four years before, he got on his knees and put his head in the dirt behind the DMV.

It comes back to him vividly, even passionately:

"The night before I'd lain in this field feeling sorry for myself. 'Sonny, you don't have a home. You don't have a job. It's cold in the winter. It's hot in the summer. How can you ever get back on your feet?'

"After I prayed, I laid there under the stars, looking up at them and saying, 'Guys, this is so cool! Isn't this beautiful? It's like camping, man. Everybody else is lying in an apartment looking at stucco. And we're lying here looking at glory.'

"That night I felt so free."

It was as if he had camped out in the city of God.

Living in Grace City

So, where do you work?" I asked, standing in the church lobby with Donte and Stephanie after weekend services.

"Uh, we're in entertainment," Donte said.

"Cool, what kind of entertainment?"

"We're both dancers."

"Great! What show do you dance in?"

"Well," he said, "we dance in different shows." It seemed like he may have wanted to change the subject, but I pressed on.

"What time are the shows and where? Lori and I may want to check them out."

"They're both pretty late," he replied. "It was great to meet you. We've gotta run.... Take care." And he and his wife bolted out the door.

I stood there reflecting on the awkwardness of the moment. I had not been in the Vegas area long and was still learning the town's dynamics. An hour later Donte drove back to the church hoping to find me, but I had already left.

The next morning I had an e-mail from Donte saying it was great to meet, and he felt bad about holding back in our conversation. He informed me that both he and Stephanie were in the adult entertainment industry. They still wanted to get together though, and we set a time to meet.

On a warm, beautiful afternoon, I made the drive to a local coffee shop. They were both there when I arrived. I immediately liked them. Donte and Stephanie are delightful people. They are intelligent, fun, and, as I soon learned, serious about their faith. They think about it, struggle with it, and share it with others. They often bring several dancers with them to church on a weekend. They seemed more intent and focused on their spiritual journey than many in more "acceptable" professions I'd met.

But I had never known people who both danced in adult shows and described themselves as serious about their faith. Questions came to mind, and as we talked, I gently probed.

Had their faith made a tangible difference in their lives? Absolutely, they said. It inspired them to be baptized, to commit to one another in marriage, and it challenged them to serve and help others.

But don't they see a conflict between what they believe and what they do for a living? Yes. They acknowledged a very real spiritual conflict, one they didn't feel good about, but one they admitted not being able to resolve. At least not yet.

After our conversation, I drove back to Central reflecting on the couple's spiritual journey. I was in turmoil. Like most committed Christians, I struggle with the idea that other self-described committed Christians could also be pursuing adult entertainment as a career. And for good reason. So-called "adult entertainment" is a convenient euphemism, after all. In Donte and Stephanie's case, it might be more accurately described as a staged event where gorgeous dancers perform naked (or nearly so) for money. However artistic or professional the performance is on the part of the dancers, the spectators are usually in it for lust.

I found myself in a spiritual wrestling match. Can an adult entertainer be a committed Christian? How could they possibly reconcile the Bible's teachings on sexuality, marriage, and personal holiness with what their jobs required? How should I as their pastor respond?

But alongside the confusion and the questions, I also felt genuinely thrilled that Donte and Stephanie were opening their lives to God, and glad they had the courage to talk with me. Where should confused and conflicted spiritual searchers be, anyway, if not in church?

Walking into my office, I glanced up at my wall where I have a large picture of the Las Vegas Valley. It was taken from the top of the Stratosphere Hotel and Casino just as the sun set. Across the orange and purple horizon are the words "Grace City." The picture reminds me that while the world may see this area as Sin City, I see something else. I see a place where grace is found and shared, where new life is experienced, where relationships are healed and hope is born. I see a city filled with people God loves. People just like Donte and Stephanie.

As a pastor committed to a conservative Christian faith, I have no reason to water down the message of Christ and what He came to accomplish. He came to free people who were—and still are—enslaved by sin, and it is my job to share that message, to call people to break free from the bondage of sin.

But after I call sin what it is, I want to be soft on people. I've learned that my assessment of others is always incomplete. Sometimes people who have it together externally are a mess internally. They hide dark secrets and addictions. I've known people who appear together on the outside, but sexually abuse their children or beat their spouse in secret. No matter how well-grounded my assessment of someone may be, it is still incomplete. So if I'm going to be wrong anyway, I choose to err on the side of grace. I choose to suppress the initial categories I want to put people in—rich, poor, together, not together, druggie, yuppie, rocker, loser, winner, cool, uncool. I choose to remember that I don't know their struggle or their pain. I choose to err on the side of grace because someday I'll stand before God, and I pray He'll err on the side of grace with me.

The truth is we are all a mess, but God loves messy people. I turn to the Bible and see Jesus hanging out with the riffraff of society. Eventually the religious leaders accused Him of being a glutton and a drunkard. He "welcomes sinners and eats with them," they said (Luke 15:2). We can't overestimate how radical this was in Jesus' culture. To share a meal meant to extend a bond of friendship. Jews never ate with those considered to be outcasts or unclean. Even today, for an orthodox Jew to have you at his table is to invite you into an experience of companionship. Eating together is a picture of acceptance, loyalty, and trust. At the table with Jesus, outcasts found a refuge, the hopeless found hope, and the oppressed found an advocate. Luke says He welcomed sinners. The term *welcome* could be translated to say He took "great pleasure" in them and felt "goodwill" toward them. I love that!

Jesus did not simply hang out with people on the fringes of society; He took great pleasure in being around them. "Sinners" referred to those of low reputation who engaged in blatant sin—prostitutes, crooked businessmen, drunks, and rough and tumble people like the ones you see on Jerry Springer. As they sat and laughed together, He imparted meaning and purpose with His presence. He blew up the social norms and celebrated life with others. All of this infuriated the religious leaders of Jesus' day.

Why did Jesus delight in these people? Certainly because they were loved by God. Perhaps also because they didn't pretend to be blameless. There is something refreshing about those who readily acknowledge imperfections. Rather than play self-righteous games, they are stripped of pride, aware of their brokenness, and open to the message of a savior. Jesus said the religious establishment was worse off because they thought they were righteous and were blind to their own sin.

Too often we mistake grace for weakness, forgiveness for giving in. We see strength only in pointing out sin and stomping on it until it's dead. But in Jesus we find someone who has no patience for those more concerned with enforcing the rules than helping others. Though He was perfect and, therefore, in a position to judge and punish all of us, Jesus showed us a different kind of strength, a strength found in grace, compassion, and forgiveness.

Jesus had a way about Him that caused people to feel they could approach Him. Children ran to Him and sat in His lap. Women were drawn to Him and His message in a culture that oppressed women. His inclusiveness shook people. He related to those of another race and religion (Samaritans), those of questionable professions, and members of the religious elite. He challenged all to love their neighbors, care for the poor, and live toward God. He showed grace to those who needed it most. But if I may be blunt, He was not a wuss.

He was strong, and He attracted strong people. Two of His closest followers were known as the "sons of thunder," implying they were loud, boisterous people. Jesus said the "kingdom of heaven has been forcefully advancing, and forceful men lay hold of it" (Matthew 11:12). He blasted religious leaders, calling them "hypocrites." And He called Herod, the ruler of the region, "that fox," meaning he was treacherous and unprincipled. He charged the temple courts and assaulted the dishonest money-changers, overthrowing their goods and driving them out. He insulted certain traditions by blatant disregard. When questioned by the religious leaders, He often responded with questions and stories that pushed buttons and probed hearts, provoking those trying to trap Him. His faith overcame fear, and He faced His enemies valiantly.

Jesus referred to Himself as the "Son of Man" or "Son of humanity." To say someone was the "son of" this or that in the ancient Middle East meant he represented those qualities to the max. We say Elvis is the "King of Rock and Roll," and to be the "King" means he represents the ideal of rock and roll. In a similar way, Jesus as the "Son of Man" embodies the best of humanity. He represents the ideal of what it means to be a complete person, while at the same time being fully God.

Jesus was also called the "Son of God," and He is our most tangible and relatable representation of God. Through Jesus I see that God is strong and loving and kind and gracious and serious and compassionate and confrontational. And I see that I should strive to be all those things too. I see a God who values honesty, truth, commitment, justice, faith, and hope. And I see that I should value those things as well.

Ultimately, Jesus' love and strength took Him to a death on the cross. Why? Because the question of sin is one of life and death. Sin kills, but God loved us enough to pay the price to rescue us from that fate. Jesus died for me. He died for adult-entertainment dancers. He died for you. Our sins drove Him to it.

So we can never stop wrestling with the seriousness of sin. And we can never stop thanking Him for the forgiveness and new life that He makes possible.

• • •

I'll be the first to acknowledge that the Good News of Jesus is easier to talk about than to live. For centuries, Christians have struggled to live out the gospel of grace in their communities. What does it *really* look like to hate the sin but love the sinner?

Jesus loved people without approving of everything they did. But for a period I didn't believe this was possible for the rest of us. I'd turn on the TV and see Christians yelling at women entering abortion clinics or protesting some moral abomination. There didn't seem to be much love going on. As soon as one started to differentiate between loving the person and disapproving of the sin, self-righteousness appeared along with plenty of hate. Then one day I read a paragraph by C. S. Lewis that rocked me. He noted that there is someone I love even though I do not always approve of what he does. There is someone I accept, though I don't like some of his actions. That someone is . . . me. I don't like my impatience toward my kids, my selfishness with my wife, or my temper when someone cuts me off on the road. I don't like it when I speak before I think and hurt others. I don't like a lot of the things I do, yet I still accept myself. I do love at least one sinner, even though I don't approve of his sin. If I can accept and love myself in this way, I can seek to extend a similar compassion to others. This insight allowed me to love people freely, irrespective of what they may or may not be doing.

The group that made Jesus angriest was the religious group known as the Pharisees. They were also the group He was most like. Both Jesus and the Pharisees obeyed the law, and Jesus often took their side in public arguments. Believers today share similarities with the Pharisees because they follow

God, seek to obey the commandments, give financially, and send out missionaries. Yet Jesus singled out these religious leaders for His strongest attacks. He called them "snakes," "a brood of vipers," "fools," "hypocrites" and "blind guides"! The Pharisees were too ready to condemn everyone else for their sins while refusing to acknowledge their own. It is easy to become part of the problem rather than the solution. As German philosopher Friedrich Nietzsche said, "Be careful, lest in fighting the dragon you become the dragon."[4]

I'm reminded of Jesus' words to the believers at Ephesus in the book of Revelation. He praises them for their deeds, perseverance, knowledge, and endurance. He notes that they don't tolerate evil and have not grown weary in the faith. Yet He has something against them for they "have forsaken [their] first love" (Revelation 2:4). This is often interpreted to mean they have lost their initial spiritual passion toward God. Yet the text literally reads, "Your first love you have left." That is quite a charge for a group that is being obedient, persevering, suffering faithfully, and not tolerating evil.

Christian scholar D. A. Carson notes the "failure of these Christians was not primarily loss of love for God but loss of love for people."[5] These believers lost love and compassion for those who are far from God. The remedy is to turn around and "do the things you did at first" (Revelation 2:5). Over thirty years earlier Paul commended the believers at Ephesus for their love for one another. Now Jesus threatens to remove their light because they do not love others. He literally threatens to step away from this church because they no longer love people. This is how serious Jesus is about us loving those from all walks of life and all corners of society.

Ephesus is not the only community to lose its love for people far from God. I've known churches where people turn their nose up at the guy who steps outside to smoke after the morning service. One person told me that after several judgmental looks and a few snide remarks, he took it as confirmation that he wasn't good enough for church or for God…and he left. He was driven away from God by the very people who were supposed to represent Him.

One friend of mine had his marriage shattered by adultery. When he reached out to the church for help, he was told he would be welcomed back to the church *after* he reconciled what happened and made it right. How does one go about doing that in isolation? Their family was in crisis, and they needed help to reconcile the situation.

Another lady said she was leaving the church because she didn't like the type of people that were showing up and she did not approve of the way they dressed. As she put it, "I'm scared to even sit in *my* seat at church because you never know what you might get from *those* people." I tend to think her comment was much more offensive to Jesus than the things *those* people were doing.

All of this brings me back to the picture on my office wall and to those words "Grace City." I look at it often and am reminded of the millions who live in the Vegas Valley and beyond. Each one of them has a story, like Sonny McKenna and Donte and Stephanie. Each one has a need for the grace of God, a grace I'm reminded of as the sun sets on the hotels and casinos, the nightclubs and strip clubs, the high-rise condos and entertainment venues, and the suburban landscape. Every day is an opportunity for a new beginning. Every day there is hope because of God's grace.

It is a beautiful irony that God is moving in a dramatic

way in America's most notorious city. Yet this is just like God; His light shines in the darkest of places. In the ancient world, the city of Corinth had similarities to Vegas. It was a tourist mecca due to its strategic location and the Isthmian Games, an event similar to the Olympics, which brought loads of tourists every two years. Corinth was based on a service economy and filled with those who supported hotels, clubs, and entertainment. Major port cities were notorious for their decadence, and Corinth shared this notoriety. Sexual immorality was rampant. One ancient writer observed that the temple of Aphrodite owned a thousand temple-slaves used for sacred prostitution.[6] Corinth was so corrupt and well-known for its sexual exploits that Aristophanes used the city's name to coin the Greek verb *korinthiazesthai*, which means "to fornicate."[7] Plato even referred to a prostitute as a "Corinthian girl."[8] And unless we begin to think that our contemporary versions of sin are new or shocking, we should consider the acceptable theatrical performance in Corinth of a woman having sex with a donkey.[9] Yet, in this city God moved in a significant way and faith thrived.

In the New Testament, we find two letters written to the believers in Corinth. Paul describes a church filled with people who are on a spiritual journey, but have not arrived. There are divisions and quarrels within the church, lawsuits among church members, disorderly conduct in the church services, sexual immorality, the abusing of communion and spiritual gifts, and a lack of maturity in general. Yet he still calls them "saints" and pleads with them as fellow believers.

He begins his first letter to the Corinthians emphasizing God's grace: "I always thank God for you because of his grace given you in Christ Jesus" (1 Corinthians 1:4). The spiritual life starts and ends with grace. Maybe that is why virtually every one of Paul's letters in the New Testament begins with "Grace be *to* you" and ends with "Grace be *with* you." The life of faith begins with grace and is sustained by grace. Grace is with us as we face a difficult boss, struggle as parents, and navigate the landmines of life. Grace is there when we sin, fail, or feel embarrassed and alone. Grace will eventually carry us home.

I'm ashamed and embarrassed that Bible-believing churches have so often failed the people God loves by holding on to judgment and refusing to show them His grace. But it doesn't have to be this way. It's time to take risks to do things differently.

Across the street from Central is a "Live Nude Adult Bookstore." At one time they had strobe lights that would shoot into the night sky, which you could see from quite a distance. People would give directions to the church and say, "Go to the strobe lights on the southeast end of the city, then turn right and the church is there." To me, it is a picture of redemption.

Go to the Live Nude Adult Bookstore and turn right.

No matter how damaged we are by life, God's grace and love are only a turn away. That's why I don't call Vegas Sin City. I call it Grace City.

PART TWO: GRACE TO BE

What Would Simon Say?

Jason's Story

Jason Walters crossed paths with *American Idol* almost on a lark. He was en route from his parents' home in Vegas back to the Virgin Islands, where he had just spent the summer working in a charter-boat business. And to get there he had to stop in New York to make plane connections on the same day as the opening of *American Idol* auditions at the Javits Convention Center in Manhattan.

Back in Vegas, one of his cousins had been pushing him to try out. After all, he did have a beautiful tenor voice, the gift of a mother who sang lullabies to him as an infant and knew every Sinatra song by heart. Jason had also graduated from the prestigious Las Vegas Academy, where every student had to demonstrate talent in song, music, or stage.

Jason had seen *Idol* on TV the season before. That was the year Ruben Studdard and Clay Aiken went down to the wire in the finals. But in his eighteen-year-old sophistication he considered the concept of the show cheesy and dumb—a kind of amateur hour for a month or two of lowbrow musical fame. Nevertheless, his cousin finally brought him around. Jason Walters would stop in New York on the way back to the islands and try out.

He caught a cab from JFK Airport after his red-eye flight from Vegas and pulled up curbside at the convention center on a Saturday morning. He had his suitcase and an airplane pillow in tow. He knew instantly he was entering a mob scene—the *American Idol* underside viewers never see.

Thousands of hopefuls lined up within barricades ahead of him and thousands more eventually queued up behind. All that day and into the night they inched and arrived, inched and arrived. He ate Chinese carryout and beef jerky dispensed by a vendor at the curb. Some people placed bed sheets over the barricades to gain the illusion of privacy. Banks of port-a-potties were maneuvered into position.

He slept that late September night on the sidewalk and nearly froze. Legions of junior *Idol* producers barked orders as their assistants, along with some New York cops, worked alongside them to keep the contestants in line. *Idol* camera crews shot people between the barricades. The contestants were reduced to cattle.

Sunday turned sweltering. Jared, the guy from the Subway TV commercials, worked the line, promoting the then-new buffalo chicken subs. Day again turned to night and still the lines got longer. But on Monday morning before daybreak, with twelve thousand people laying their heads on concrete, overnight bags, or even other bodies, came the heavenly call: "Up and at 'em! You're goin' in!"

It took five hours for Jason to get through the processing. Then he sat in an auditorium with no instructions for upwards of four hours. His stopover was quickly becoming an odyssey.

He knew nothing about the underside of *American Idol.* What he had seen the previous season was big Ruben edging out Clay. That and the three judges—Simon Cowell, Paula Abdul, and Randy Jackson—weeding out the loons and attention seekers, whose only dream was a fleeting few seconds on camera, from the real *Idol* talent.

Jason now learned there were two distinct audition rounds he had to survive before gaining the right to appear in front of Simon, Paula, and Randy.

The first was an audition at one of twelve makeshift booths, each manned by two producers who rendered snap judgments on the convention center floor. Jason and three other contestants each sang a few lines of a song at his assigned booth.

In *American Idol* everything rides on this first brief appearance.

Jason's selection was "Unchained Melody" by the Righteous Brothers. When he was through, one of the producers, a British woman, asked for something faster. He sang a riff from Al Green's "Let's Stay Together." It wasn't easy to stay on pitch amidst the bedlam. Contestants were singing loudly and simultaneously at all the eleven other booths, each side by side on the floor.

When Jason was through, the British judge said, "I'm going to keep you and you." She pointed at him and a woman in her twenties who had been off pitch, was grossly overweight, and generally evoked pity. It was then that Jason understood *Idol's* method of including "cows" and "mules," as the insiders call them. Chosen by assistant producers, they serve in the early rounds as pathetically delightful foils for the judges on television.

But Jason had survived the first huge cut. He posed for his official photo holding contestant card No. 46067. Of the twelve thousand hopefuls who showed up in New York, only five hundred were left. He was happy, but not as excited as you might think. He had just been living in a Caribbean paradise and now had to schlep around Manhattan, carrying his suitcase, looking for a hotel and some new clothes to wear. In the islands he could drink and smoke pot every day. In Manhattan he didn't know where to get a stash.

The next New York audition rounds were held at the famously elegant Waldorf-Astoria hotel. When Jason called home to his mother, she sprung for a more than $400-per-night room for the rest of the competition. He went to Macy's on 34th Street and had the men's department outfit him in a deep blue dress shirt and smart black trousers.

His next *Idol* step was not before a midlevel producer but in front of Nigel Lythgoe and Ken Warwick, *American Idol*'s executive producers and top bosses. After waiting with other contestants in a banquet hall for almost a day, he was called into a room before them and again sang "Unchained Melody."

Lythgoe and Warwick told him he needed to work on his facial expressions and shave the goatee he had grown.

They obviously liked him, though, because they passed him into the next round of 250. This guaranteed him an appearance before Simon, Paula, and Randy within the next two days—one that might make an *American Idol* TV installment four months later, after the editing had been done.

When the contestants had waited almost a full day, Simon came out of the judging room with Paula, Randy, and Ryan Seacrest, the famous *Idol* emcee.

"Listen," Simon said, "if you think you sound like Frank Sinatra, Madonna, or Stevie Wonder, you shouldn't be here. If you think that they sound like *you*, then welcome to *American Idol*. We want original. Don't try to impersonate—that's not what we want."

The reference to Sinatra rattled Jason. After all, there had been moments in the shower when he thought he did sound quite a bit like Old Blue Eyes.

An hour later Jason was called on deck before the TV cameras to a hallway outside a conference room where the judging would occur. He gargled with Listerine to clear his vocal cords as he normally does before he sings and emptied it into a Styrofoam cup.

D-Day. Suddenly it was time.

An attendant pulled open the door and Jason walked inside onto a tiny stage about twenty feet in front of the judges.

Randy quickly asked him the number he planned to sing.

"Unchained Melody," Jason said.

"Oh, now listen," Randy said. "Let me warn you—are you really good?" It was Randy's way of needling Jason—the song was famous for being one of Simon's favorites.

"Oh, yeah, I believe that I am—yes," Jason said.

"Look who he played for…" Paula said, glancing at Jason's bio sheet in front of her at the judging table.

"He played for who?" Randy said.

"The Pope."

"The Pope? Wow… "

"And President and Mrs. Clinton for their Christmas press tour," Paula added.

"Wow!" Randy said. "Very good, dude, go with it…"

As Jason sang, Simon sat straight-faced, rotating a pencil between his index fingers. When the few bars were over, Randy, looking noncommittal and serious, said, "Okay, it's all right. Paula, what do you think?"

She smiled in an "I'm intrigued" kind of way. "I think he has a future and did a very nice job. What can you say? I think he has a very nice voice."

"Simon Cowell, your favorite song," Randy said, setting him up.

"One of the best versions I've ever heard," Simon said. "In the beginning part of that song, he was literally note perfect."

"Well, guess what?" Randy said to Jason. "Welcome to Hollywood, Dawg!"

Though he was only eighteen, Jason had already traveled a long road to Hollywood.

Born in Orchard Park, New York, near Buffalo, he moved to Vegas with his mom, Rosann; his dad, Mike; and his older sister, Krista, when he was ten. The Vegas boom was in full flower in the nineties with thousands of new homes going up each year in suburban Henderson, where the Walterses settled.

Jason's talent was evident early. He joined the Las Vegas Academy's children's choir in seventh grade, mastered all of Sinatra's greatest hits over the next two years, and gained admission to the Academy's magnet high school near Fremont Street by auditioning with "The Way You Look Tonight."

"I was a bit of a prep, but maybe a little too comfortable with the opposite sex at a very young age," he says. By graduation he was a party animal.

Then he left home for the first time, having gained entry to the California Institute of the Arts, the prestigious college near Los Angeles founded by Walt Disney. It was a dynamic move for most students, but an all but disastrous one for him.

Jason had tried pot in Vegas. But his Cal Arts roommate, later kicked out of a dorm there for possession of it, had a supply line unknown to the school authorities. He and Jason began smoking together daily. They stepped up to mixing pot, beer, and alternate shots of whiskey with others on their floor.

"We were punks," Jason now says with chagrin. After resident advisors on the floor eventually smelled the pot and found the roommate's stash, the school barred him from the dorm. Jason avoided the same penalty because it wasn't his pot. But he knew his number would eventually be up, and he left Cal Arts after just one year.

"I was into pot so bad," he says, "that I had my parents come pick me up rather than catch a flight back home for Christmas break. They didn't know why—that I just wanted to bring my stash back with me and couldn't risk airport security. If we had been stopped on the road, my parents would probably have said it was theirs and taken the heat for me. How stupid!"

That June, three months before he would audition for *Idol,* Jason's sister invited him to the Virgin Islands, where she had been living with her boyfriend for half a year on St. Thomas. Bored at home, motivated by little except finding his next reefer and partying with his Vegas friends, he decided to go. All he wanted to do was make enough money to be stoned half the time, just as he had been at Cal Arts.

In the Caribbean, his first mission was to find a personal pot supplier.

He hooked up with the fortysomething owner of a small charter-boat company. Jason and his boss, Maurice, would start smoking by noon and spend the rest of the day stoned. Then they would drink so much in the evening they would all but pass out.

He lived like a feather on the breeze. His aimlessness became his signature statement.

"I'd wake up every morning and think, *Yeah, how cool is this, not many people get to do what I'm doing,*" he recalls. "I knew I couldn't stay there forever. But it was one of those periods just floating. I didn't have a lot of plans for my life. ...e, *Well, I'm here now, aren't I?*"

Jason's job, such as it was, required him to zip around the island in the owner's Jeep, schmoozing with hotel staffers who might send business the boat company's way. He would routinely make his afternoon rounds high. He wore sunglasses so no one could tell he'd been smoking.

"It got to the point where you could cope," he recalls. "You could walk around to the concierges, and as long as you had sunglasses on they wouldn't know.

"My sister said, 'If you've got to smoke, go out on the porch—I don't want it inside.' I was out drinking every night. I was home early, but I was drunk. I can't even tell you what happened on certain nights. Either high or drunk, everything ran together.

"I can tell you some things that happened in St. Thomas. But can I tell you when things happened and in what order? I don't think so. There's memory loss with that kind of living."

"Welcome to Hollywood!" Randy had said.

"Hollywood," however, turned out to be Pasadena, about ten miles away, where *American Idol* had taken over an aging theater for the next round of judging.

Jason was now back from St. Thomas, after a month and a half of boozing, for the next stage of *Idol's* competition—the notoriously grueling Hell Week. It's actually just a three-day stretch. But it's one in which hundreds of contestants are thrown together, deprived of sleep, beckoned to perform at a moment's notice, told to be totally silent for hours at a time while recording is underway, and forced to write and perform songs with "partners" they have known for just half a day.

Jason calls it "boot camp for singers." The first two days consisted of sudden auditions before Simon, Paula, and Randy, or other high-level *Idol* producers. On the first night, each contestant was required to sing a song of his or her choice *a cappella*. It was nerve-racking—all the more so because there wasn't a word of feedback from the judges.

Jason had not practiced for even one hour back in the islands. Others needed to work on their voice, but singing had always been a snap for him.

The contestants slept in seats at the theater. No frills.

Day two dawned.

Producers called the hopefuls to attention in the morning and gave each a short phrase. The assignment was to write a verse and chorus of a song incorporating all the words. Each contestant would have to memorize the song and sing it for the judges the following morning. The producers' only advice: "Write something that reflects your personality."

Jason's phrase happened to be "Ten reasons why I'm leaving you."

"I wrote this cheesy Adam Sandler-esque kind of song about having a girlfriend who leaves me for my trainer at the gym," he recalls.

When the next morning came, Jason's adrenaline was flowing. Randy thought his performance was "just okay, dude." Simon thought he "had issues" about some girlfriend that must have left him. But none of the judges ran down the quality of his voice—a moral victory.

Late that night the cuts were about to be made. Of the 127 scrungy *Idol* hopefuls waiting in four separate meeting rooms to hear their fate, some sixty would be going home.

Unknown to the contestants, the sixty about to be canned had all been herded into one room. The sixty-seven survivors had been evenly divided among the other three rooms.

Simon, Paula, and Randy came into Jason's room stone-faced, if not gloomy. All the contestants in the room were glum as well—and for good reason. They had just heard three separate cheers erupting from the other contestants' rooms. It obviously was all over for them.

Simon called everyone to attention.

"I'm sorry to tell you this…" he said, pausing to milk the drama. "But you have all made it to the next round."

The room exploded with emotion. Jason leapt off his feet and threw a fist in the air. There was shouting and rejoicing. The *Idol* producers had played a little trick on them to make their joyous reactions that much more pronounced—and that much better for the cameras.

At any rate, "Walters, Jason, No. 46067" had survived for another day.

But Jason still had to dodge two more bullets. The sixty-seven still alive would be reduced to an intermediate group of fifty. Then that group would be cut to thirty-two—the final field that would advance to the finals on TV.

Day two blended into day three. The exhausted finalists now were told to form groups of three among themselves. Every contestant was required to pick one of three songs, each with a different tempo, and scout around the hall to form trios with others who had picked the same one. The task for each trio was to memorize a verse and a chorus and prepare to perform by seven o'clock that morning.

Jason's group selected "Up on the Roof," the old Drifters song later recorded by James Taylor. After being on edge throughout day two, the trio now practiced their parts until 3 a.m., catching a few hours sleep before the seven o'clock deadline.

But the morning deadline came and passed in the large old theater. No producers. No Simon, Paula, or Randy. Hours more passed. Exhaustion was setting in.

"We had it memorized that morning," Jason remembers. "But by the afternoon I was forgetting this phrase here and that word there. I was saying to myself, *Oh no, I'm losing it!* They don't show on TV how grueling the process is. And you can't really understand it until you get there. It's crazy."

In midafternoon, Warwick, the co-executive producer, and some of his associates arrived.

"Guys," Warwick said, "don't worry about this day. This is just to get the judges to hear your voice again. Don't worry that much about the words to your song because it really doesn't matter to them."

A short while later Simon and Randy came in. Before taking their places in front of the stage they offered a final word to all contestants.

"Guys," Simon said, "the most important thing about today is...*do not forget your words.*"

Most contestants looked at each other quizzically. *Say what???*

Jason's group was the second onto the stage.

"I don't think it was necessarily my nerves so much as sheer exhaustion," he remembers. "When you're that early going before the judges, you can't learn from anybody's mistakes. It's all about the mistakes you make, and then people learn from you.

"We started singing and I forgot some of the words. We all were singing, of course, and I still didn't sound bad, but I kind of mumbled some of the words."

After about three more hours, a few *Idol* underlings emerged and read from a short list of cuts. Jason and his partners had bit the dust.

He had finished about sixtieth among the tens of thousands of singers who auditioned. His reaction? Overwhelming fatigue. It was as if all the adrenaline that carried him for so long had evaporated in a nanosecond.

The underlings gave Jason a chance to have a few final words with the judges.

"Simon," he said, "I thought you said I sang one of the best versions you'd ever heard of your favorite song…"

Simon was in no mood for engagement. It was vintage Simon.

"I remember," he said succinctly.

Jason didn't return to St. Thomas after his *Idol* ride abruptly ended. He simply journeyed home and went back to his pot. He preferred lying around the house and smoking to the rigors of pursuing a job.

"It wasn't that I was down about not making *Idol*," he says. "It was the fact I was no longer in the Caribbean. I had left the islands to pursue something that didn't work out. And now I was back in the house without that freedom because I was living with my parents."

There were jobs to be had stacking pallets at Home Depot, but he couldn't have cared less. Self-motivation had always been a problem for him, and now he just hunkered down in his room with his pot while his father, a diabetic, and grandmother sat around. His mother, the worker bee, didn't want him smoking in her house and told him so. *But what*, Jason thought, *she's going to force me out on the street?*

While Jason was listless and stoned, the work he did in the *American Idol* auditions started to pay off.

Two or three years before, while he was at Las Vegas

Academy, Jason had dated a girl named Amanda Quillen. They were an item for a season, but eventually the relation- ship ended.

Not long after Jason auditioned for *Idol*, Amanda happened to be watching one of the *American Idol* prelim shows. She was stunned to see him performing before Simon, Paula, and Randy. And not long after she watched Randy say, "Welcome to Hollywood, Dawg," she was on the phone to Jason.

They talked several more times, met, and gradually became friends again.

It was different for Jason this time, perhaps because of his father. Mike Walters by now had lost half a leg and part of a foot to diabetes and suffered three strokes that further incapacitated him. It was a reality check for his son.

A month or two after they saw each other again, Amanda invited Jason to Central's weekly service.

Jason was raised Catholic, and of all four members of his family he was the one most interested in things spiritual. He made his First Communion and attended church school as a child, but then drifted. When he was sixteen he "walked the aisle" at a friend's Southern Baptist church—an outward sign of conversion.

But "receiving Christ" seemed more like the thing to do at the time than an encounter with reality. "I was young, acting stupid," he says. And then came the year devoted to pot smoking at Cal Arts and the lost summer in St. Thomas.

Now, with his *American Idol* dream over, with his father having lost his health, he related to Central on a different level. The second week they were there Jason found himself asking Christ to take over his life.

"My family thought I had done it for Amanda, but the truth was I did it for me," he says.

Jason's faith had somehow given him the power to leave the pot and the heavy booze behind. He took a short course at the church on the essentials of Christianity and soon was baptized as an adult.

As it turned out, Jason wasn't through with *American Idol*. But he found himself growing beyond it.

Idol held one of its cattle-call auditions in Vegas at the Orleans Arena on Tropicana. Jason by then was attending Las Vegas Community College and working at the Fairfield Grand Desert Resort. He decided to try out again.

For the first round of auditions at the booth, some mid-level producers recognized him and said they had hoped he would come back. He polished his renditions of Elton John's "Can You Feel the Love Tonight?" and Billy Joel's "For the Longest Time."

Another woman was his judge.

"Good job, you're through," she told him after a few bars of "Longest Time."

His next stop was before Lythgoe and Warwick, the executive producers. He sang "Feel the Love" and was again encouraged. Not only did the head honchos remember him, they were almost flattering. They seemed puzzled why he had failed to make it.

"Just do what you did last time," Warwick said, "and you'll probably be okay."

Unlike in New York, Jason was able to get a number and sleep at home instead of on the sidewalk. But this time he faced a crisis. His father had fallen into a diabetic coma the week of the competition. Doctors didn't know whether he would survive. Jason's mother wanted him to continue on *Idol*, but he was hardly the center of his family's concern.

This time he prayed before walking in before the judges.

"Lord," he said, "if it's me making it onto *American Idol* or my dad waking up, you know which one I want more."

The audition before the judges was at the MGM Grand Conference Center, a block from the Strip. Simon, Paula, and Randy recognized him when he entered. And the latter two allowed that when they recently watched the tapes from the previous year, Jason sounded better to them than he had originally. Kenny Loggins, the singer and songwriter, had joined the panel as a guest judge.

Jason was going to go with "Can You Feel the Love Tonight" or Billy Joel's "For the Longest Time." He chose the Elton John number at the last moment.

"Looking back," Jason says, "I don't think I was really with it when I got in front of the judges. I had so much on my mind—especially that day, worrying about my dad. Part of it was me thinking, *My father's life is on the line, he's my only father, and here I am singing.* It just really wasn't as important as I thought."

When he was through, a debate began.

"Paula and Randy went off on how they really didn't like me from the previous year because I was too old-fashioned in my singing," Jason recalls.

Simon then said, "Yes, you *are* old-fashioned." But he stood up for him. "Paula," Simon said, "you liked him from last year when you watched the tapes back, didn't you?"

Loggins now interjected: "Elton John doesn't just sing but really expresses his words of music to his audience. I didn't feel it as much from you. I have to say no."

Randy chimed in: "Nada, not for me."

Paula said, "No, too old-fashioned."

Simon pitched in his hand. "Well, I guess you're not going to Hollywood this year," he concluded.

Jason and his mother are unsure of the timing, but about the moment he was voted out, his father emerged from his coma after a little less than a week.

Without speaking to Jason, his mother felt sure he had not advanced and that it was all okay. Jason called from the MGM with the report of what had happened and was greeted with the news about his dad.

A few years removed from his *American Idol* dreams, Jason Walters has discovered more of who he is. He found his identity not in the fame and applause of *Idol*, nor in the whirlwind pursuit of having more, nor in the dead-end desire to party harder. He found value in a relationship with God. He rests in that security and hope. It has changed everything about his life and how he views himself.

Jason sits at a table in his home and examines the what ifs. What if the show's producers had not decided to use the tape of his first audition before Simon, Paula, and Randy on national TV the following spring? Then Amanda would never have seen him, would never have called...

What if Amanda had never invited him to Central? He may never have entered into a deep relationship with Christ... And in that case, he would never have been singing in the church's weekend services... And he would never have been taking a series of theology courses toward a degree in the ministry... And he would never have married Amanda.

"I'm a big believer that everything is meant to be for a reason," he says.

"Looking back at *American Idol*, it was pretty much a

fluke. I didn't practice to get on the show. I just showed up and did it. Maybe getting as far as I did but no further taught me to be a little more humble. Maybe it taught me I'm going to have to work for the things I get.

"You're saved by faith and not by works, but you do have to work at Christianity afterward. You have to work to turn your life around. Stopping smoking pot—that was a narrow road for me. But I took it.

"And I just wonder if I had gone on and not been around for my dad...

"My father came close"—Jason holds up his thumb and forefinger with only a centimeter between them to illustrate just how close—"but now he has accepted Christ. He turned his life around in the last couple of years."

How do you weigh advancing on *Idol* against finding purpose and harmony in one's life? God has a way of ending some dreams in the process of fulfilling others.

"Thank You, Thank You Very Much"

Brian's Story

Even when the mob held sway, back in the fifties and sixties, Vegas was becoming an Elvis kind of town. It was already the place for rhinestones, extravagant costumes, and outsized personalities. In some respects Liberace, playing the new Riviera with his glittering jackets and beautiful hair and sweet purring voice, was a Presley precursor—if only for aging blue-haired ladies.

Before he became an overnight idol by appearing on *The Ed Sullivan Show* (though only from the waist up), Elvis also did Vegas. He was booked at the Venus Room of the New Frontier Hotel and Casino on the Strip. In front of the hotel's main entrance stood a twenty-four-foot-high cutout of the twenty-one-year-old star.

Elvis and his rockabilly band wound up bombing in the Venus Room. He was before his time in Vegas, which then catered to an older, more traditional crowd. As Vegas historian Hal Rothman has put it, Elvis was then "the fringe, and Las Vegas only did well with the center."[10]

But sensibilities were changing.

After his rise to fame, after "All Shook Up," after his hitch in the army and the movie "Viva Las Vegas," a more mature Elvis returned to town. Kirk Kerkorian had hired him to perform in his new International Hotel, later to become the Hilton and at the time the largest hotel in the world. Elvis performed two shows a night for two months a year from 1969 to 1977—more than one thousand straight sell-outs in all, for $125,000 a week.

And this time he *became* Vegas.

All the Elvis mannerisms imitated after his death by two generations of Elvis impersonators were on display. The scarves, drenched in his sweat, were tucked inside his shirt ready to be distributed to adoring women at the stage. His series of shows lasted long enough for a star to become a Vegas legend.

A writer for *Life* magazine perfectly captured the phenomenon.

"What was he wearing? Nothing lavish, my dear, just a smashing white jump suit, slashed to the sternum and lovingly fitted around his broad shoulders, flat belly, narrow hips and...well, it's a nice fit. And then there are his pearls—loads of lustrous pearls, not sewn on his costume but worn unabashedly as body ornaments...

"With his massive diamonds flashing pinks and purples from his fingers and his boyish smile flashing sheepishly through his huge shag of shiny, black hormone hair, Elvis looked like a heaping portion of male cheesecake ripe for the eyeteeth of hundreds of women ogling him through opera glasses.... The number ends abruptly with Presley snapping into profile and thrusting his guitar bayonet-style at the chorus."

And so the legend was born. Elvis sometimes grabbed a woman spectator at ringside at the end of his show and kissed her firmly on the mouth. And *Life*'s man said, "Women in the audience lunge[d] toward the stage like salmon up a falls…"[11]

A celebratory crowd is gathered on a weekend evening in Vegas or its suburbs. The occasion can be anything from a large wedding to a pre-race NASCAR party or a corporate anniversary. Often the sun is beginning to set and the tinkling of glasses can be heard over half an acre of verandas and open gardens.

"Whoa!" someone gasps. "Look up there—up in the sky!"

At first a single parachutist can be seen—then two, then three, then an entire ten-man team, dots against the magenta Nevada sunset, steadily descending from more than two miles up.

"Wow!" someone at the party exclaims as the first jumper reaches one thousand feet. "I don't believe this! Hey, look at this! These guys are coming to us—they're going to land right here!!"

Brian Balducci, point man for the Flying Elvi, touches down first. He comes in quick, hits the ground, and rolls into a PLF—parachute landing fall—a military maneuver that cushions the impact and keeps him from tearing a ligament or twisting an ankle. An Elvi ground member breaks open a canister sending a wide, thin screen of smoke into the sky and silhouetting the remaining divers as they descend.

"Hound Dog" suddenly blasts from speakers on the ground. The crowd closes in on the landing site, which the ground members have quickly worked to secure. The site is everything—potentially a life-and-death decision because it must be seventy-five feet wide in all directions and free of power lines.

Jumper after jumper arrives now at twenty- to forty-second intervals. They're all Elvis impersonators, and they all wear identical Elvi uniforms: white rhinestone jumpsuits with the obligatory turned-up collar and belled sleeves that unsnap at the ends. Long bell-bottom pants with red slashes that come up to the knee. Scarlet scarves that whip in the breeze. And a mini helmet originally covered with hot glue, dyed black, and finely grooved, making it appear from thirty feet like the "shiny, black hormone hair" that *Life* so sexily described.

When all ten Elvi have landed, it's party time.

A small stage has been secured in the midst of the celebration. With all eyes upon them, the Elvi dash to it, grab their guitars, and start lip-synching to music blaring from the speakers. The crowd surges forward. The Elvi dance and swivel to the beat.

At some locations the crowd gets so hyped it's as if they're gazing upon Elvis in the flesh. The Elvi are thinking, *No, no, get real!* They call themselves impersonator-imposters, though they're not even close. But the crowds want autographs. They want pictures with the Elvi. It's a King thing and a Vegas thing.

Brian's personal shtick is to immediately take center stage and lip-synch a blaring "Don't Be Cruel." He also does some "Teddy Bear" and "Jailhouse Rock." By now he's dressed in a black wig with a clump of hair falling Elvis-like onto his forehead.

As the chief Elvis does "Fools Fall in Love," Brian begins a scarves routine, draping them around the necks of women at the stage. Then come the tympani and the cannons, shooting confetti into the crowd. Finally, the cannons boom a farewell.

The excitement is palpable.

In the movie *Honeymoon in Vegas* with Nicholas Cage, James Caan, and Sarah Jessica Parker, a skydiving team of

Elvises appeared in a climactic scene. But those Elvises later folded after one of their members was killed and others were injured when their chutes were blown into a yacht club during a jump.

Later the official "Flying Elvi" were founded in agreement with Priscilla Presley, the King's widow, and they soon became a nationwide act. Brian, a blue-collar tough guy just out of the Marines, joined the team and began jumping across the country with the others.

The tragedy involving the movie team pointed up the risks in skydiving. Brian himself has lost three friends while diving, and another Elvis was seriously injured in 2006. The most recent fatality was when Brian and a friend were out practice-jumping. It was a nightmarish case of "bag lock"—the friend's main chute never deployed. He pulled his reserve, but it then got tangled in the main chute. He came to earth with a jumble of nylon above his head and hit the ground at 120 miles an hour.

Brian the daredevil gets butterflies in his stomach and clammy palms every time he goes up in an airplane. But it's not about the jumping. "It's the takeoffs that bother me," he says. "It's because I'm not in control. Believe me, takeoffs are where we're the most vulnerable. Anything higher than a thousand feet, I can get out of the airplane through an open door."

About one in twenty-five thousand sky dives results in death. Skydivers generally leap from their plane at nine thousand to twelve thousand feet and free-fall for most of it at speeds ranging up to 160 miles an hour. Far below, huge swaths of land look like tiny postage stamps.

Brian's closest call in his thousands of jumps came when he was skysurfing on a small board attached to his feet at four thousand feet. Suddenly one foot came out of its binding and the board shot up near his chest. His main chute then opened between his legs, entangling him. He was spinning, seeing now blue sky and now the earth below. He pulled his reserve chute, but it opened only halfway and couldn't get enough air.

"I just knew I was dead," Brian recalls. "All I could think of was my son."

At last both chutes opened halfway at three hundred feet. He had just enough air and just enough chute for a clean landing.

But usually it's not so bad, and whatever anxiety exists gets swallowed up by the festive Elvi atmosphere.

"There's a little bit of fear because halfway down we might be looking at a parking lot," he says, "and it's one-quarter the size of a bottle cap. But there's so much more added to it. You might have seventy thousand people watching you. And I'm the first guy down, which always is a kick."

In their fifteen years of relative fame, Brian and the other Elvi have jumped into major theme parks and sports arenas, Fortune 500 conventions, and casino openings around the country. They've hit hotel debuts, fairs, car races, and yes, the Rock and Roll Hall of Fame. As for TV, they've made it onto *Live with Regis and Kelly*, *A Current Affair*, *Inside Edition*, *Good Morning America*, CNN, and ESPN.

What group of gonzos could be more typically Vegas?

Brian Balducci was first and foremost a tough guy. Prided himself on it. Loved the image. Could not have cared less what anyone else wanted to do.

They say that Elvis had a tender, even spiritual side growing up. In that regard, Brian was the anti-Elvis. There was nothing warm and cuddly about him.

He was raised in New Bedford, Massachusetts, a blue-collar gateway to the Atlantic Ocean. It was a weather-beaten town whose best days had come half a century before. Brian's mom and dad divorced when he was four. There were three children, and when his mother soon remarried, Brian and his stepdad were like oil and water. There was a pattern of abuse, and in Brian's teenaged years, physical fights were not uncommon between the two of them.

Brian went to a vocational tech school, learning how to refinish cars. He fashioned himself a stud, wearing tight T-shirts, standing against walls with his thumbs tucked inside his belt. He wasn't somebody you'd want your daughter to be dating. By seventeen he was out of the house—off to Parris Island, South Carolina, to join the Marines and get away from the dysfunction at home.

Brian was stronger than most recruits and had an air of assurance about him. Even though Parris Island was notorious for its discipline, he once grinned when a drill instructor got in his face. "Sir," he exclaimed, "my mom could body slam you, sir!" He actually had the nerve to show the D.I. some pictures of his mother, a half-marathoner who worked out with weights.

If he wanted to get away from bad relationships, Brian's four-year hitch in the Marines worked better than he might have imagined.

He rose only to E-4, corporal level, but for six months at a time he was stationed on Navy ships in the Caribbean and Mediterranean. He'd secure beaches and set up offload sites for simulated maneuvers. On the side, he became a pistol coach and water survival specialist, training noncommissioned officers.

The relational side of his life, though, was a sinkhole.

Back in the states while he was on duty at Camp Lejeune, North Carolina, he had been dating a woman who had three kids from a former marriage. They had been together for six months when she got pregnant with his child. What to do? Active duty was staring him in the face.

They decided to get married, and a short while later his son was born. A month or so after that he was assigned overseas.

Three years passed with the couple essentially apart. When Brian came home for good, he moved the entire family to Vegas, where his natural father had a flooring business. Brian and his blended family set up home in a lackluster house on the northeastern side of town, not far from the Air Force base.

A line in Brian's New Bedford high school yearbook listed his goals in life: "Join the Marines. Then move to Las Vegas."

His dreams had come true. But now what?

He was twenty-one and all but abusing his wife's kids, constantly punishing them, always spanking them.

"I was nasty," he recalls. "I was evil. After I got out of the Marine Corps I wanted to beat everybody up. Nobody could talk to me. I resented the kids and resented her. And when I resented her, I took it out on the kids again—it was a power thing."

The marriage, if you can call it that, lasted five years.

To fill the void, he threw himself into work, helping his father in the flooring business while also supervising work crews for the union. And with the extra time and money he suddenly had, he tried skydiving, making his first jump into an empty desert. He lined up eleven of his friends to join him—and every one of them canceled. Only his father had the nerve to come and watch.

Soon he was also working as a bouncer at Mandalay Bay's

House of Blues. He was a tough guy with a mouth and a build to match, so punks and wise guys were no match for him. He would grab the drunks by the belt and the back of their shirt, use their head to help open the door, and toss them out onto the sidewalk.

"Every night there would be trouble, and I looked forward to that—it would be my stress relief," he says. "We would fight every night, and that was okay. But using their heads to open doors.… "

He shakes his head. "Every person I did that to, I now wish I could get in a room and apologize to."

The tough guy began skydiving regularly in the desert north of Vegas in the early nineties with a few blokes who had made it into the *Honeymoon in Vegas* movie. He loved it from the get-go, even though the pals he invited always chickened out. When the Elvi were formed as rivals to the Flying Elvises, Brian happened to be jumping for kicks with one of the new group's organizers. He was fearless and he was a stud, and in short order he was invited to join the Elvi.

They were flying around America up to forty weekends a year then, compared with ten weekends today, and Brian's was the life of a mini rock star. It wasn't just about the adrenaline rush of free-falling toward the lights below. It was about hitting on women in the hotel bar. Doing shots. Talking up the most attractive girls. Collecting numbers. Working toward a one-night stand with someone he had chosen as his quarry.

He often was successful but came away feeling empty. And the meaninglessness spilled over into his relationships with women back in Vegas. He had live-in arrangements with four others after his divorce, but each relationship lasted just three or four years. It was maddening. Like clockwork the intimacy would be gone, and he'd find himself dead inside.

Why was it always like this? Was he cursed?

Sometimes Brian would just pack up and leave when the girlfriend wasn't there—the surgical strike. Other times he and the girlfriend would argue incessantly until a bigger blowup became inevitable.

His fourth relationship was with a good and caring woman named Janet. Brian was thirty-seven. They had been together for three years, but increasingly Janet seemed to want to do things that weren't at the top of Brian's interest list. The problem was that *he* was always at the top of his list. If it wasn't about him, he was flat-out not interested. He didn't take part in conversations that didn't involve him.

Brian's friends were the skydivers, the Harley-Davidson guys like himself, the grunts he drank beer with on Friday night.

"Guys in a way are kind of knuckleheads," he says today. "When it comes to relationships, they don't get it. If you don't want to do something they want to do, then get lost.

"I was a jerk. I admit it. I was just very not-caring."

After three years in their relationship, everything was becoming clearer. Janet was patient while Brian was impatient. If they were leaving the parking lot after a concert, Brian would creep up so other cars couldn't squeeze in. This seemed unkind to Janet, but a normal part of life to Brian. He would even give them his favorite one-fingered salute as he edged by. Sometimes he got out of his truck to intimidate them. Janet didn't appreciate that, but Brian loved it. *Just mess with me*, he thought.

His selfishness was at the core. If he and Janet were going to the movies, it had to be what *he* wanted to see. If they were going to be with friends, it had to be *their* friends—he wasn't about to go out with only hers.

Janet passionately wanted to go to Disneyland. He wouldn't take her. *I don't want to go, so why should I go?* With Brian there was no sacrifice, no demilitarized zone. It was all about him, first, last, and always.

Eventually Janet started attending Central.

Brian was neutral about her going initially. *Fine*, he thought. *If it can do her some good, more power to her.* She became quite active for awhile, worshiping on Sundays and attending groups and classes three nights a week. Finally the church started to impinge on her time with him. "What is this?" Brian asked. "Some sort of cult? They've got you brain-washed?"

But she seemed excited about what was happening there. And a few weeks later, somewhat out of character, he joined her on a Sunday morning. The message touched on some issues that had been dividing them. And at one point their eyes met because the content so obviously related to his self-centeredness.

Brian and Janet soon broke up, but he started attending a night class on relationships at church. One night a big guy—he looked like a pro wrestler—sat down at a table next to him. He started telling Brian about his problems—trouble with his girlfriend, hooked on heroin, lost his job, lost his car—and suddenly started bawling.

Brian began giving the guy advice on how he himself was handling things in his life. What chutzpah! By the second week, Brian was in a roomful of couples, feeling odd being one of the few single guys. But he found himself able to open up for the first time. That in itself was a breakthrough.

In the weeks that followed, he sat and listened. He came to a few conclusions—obvious in hindsight, but revelations to him at the time. For one thing, he learned that he was truly selfish. For another, he didn't enjoy being that way. And despite his self-centeredness, he did find a measure of delight when he included himself in other people's lives.

He started looking for signs from God in the pain he was feeling over the breakup with Janet. He went through weeks of a questioning phase—*Why, God, are You doing this to me? What have I done to You? Why do I need to feel all this pain and hurt?*

The first answer he seemed to get back was not what he wanted to hear: He needed to learn more about himself. The second was he needed to learn more about God—only that way could he become a better person for himself and his *next* relationship. He took a class that covered the basics of the Bible and faith in Christ. And it offered pointers on how to study and pray.

When he had prayed a few weeks before, he had been asking about stuff for himself—*God, I need to get back with Janet… God, how come this hasn't happened?… God, why can't You make it happen?*

He had been doing all the right things. Calling her five times a day and bugging her about reuniting. Sharing the merits of togetherness. Spelling out how he was going to act and what he was going to do. And for what? The more he was in her face, the angrier she seemed to become.

Now, from out of the blue, came the thought that certain people needed space more than he needed togetherness. Brian found himself getting down on his knees at the side of his bed. He was an unemotional guy and this was a highly unusual position. But on this night, the unemotional guy began to cry.

"I'm not asking You for us to get back together," he prayed. "I love this woman. And I'm hurting. If I'm supposed to let it go because we're not meant to be together, just tell me. Show me what I'm supposed to do. Because, right now, I'm doing all the wrong things."

Before these encounters, Brian had never prayed to God on a personal level. He thought God had done His work of creation, then quickly wiped His hands of the job and forgot about the humans.

So why on his knees?

"I don't know. I just knew I had to do something. I just needed to let go and have Him handle some of my problems."

Within a few weeks he began to see himself as if in a mirror. He came face-to-face with his selfishness. He identified the anger that had consumed him for much of his lifetime. He wasn't very proud of himself. But he gradually came to realize he was not alone—his was the human condition; millions of others were wrestling with the same stuff. He found comfort in knowing he wasn't alone.

It is a year or two after Brian Balducci found God.

He is sitting on a patio in the southern foothills overlooking Vegas, talking about his huge 1700-cubic centimeter Harley. Talking about his latest Ford pickup, new every three years. Talking about his life as an Elvis.

The conversation gets around to how being an Elvis is much the same as being a rock star—the make-believe becoming reality. It leaves him amazed at times.

Not long ago the Elvis impersonators flew cross-country to Florida and skydived next door to the Seminole Hard Rock Hotel & Casino in Tampa. After the show and the autograph lines, Brian put his bags in his room and came down to the bar, where some of the Elvi had congregated. A number of women fans joined them. The show continued seamlessly from the stage to the bar.

Brian had a beer, scouted out the gift shop, came back, and had another beer. As usual, the girls were hanging with the Elvi, exchanging phone numbers and soaking up the atmosphere. For Brian, the bar scene was usually one of the more enjoyable things about being an Elvis.

But on this occasion he went back up to his room and watched a movie.

Within half an hour the guys called him from the bar.

"What's up?" they said. "Come on down, man!"

"I said, 'You know what? I'm gonna pack it in.' It was just not appealing to me anymore. I have nothing against the guys, but I would have been disrespecting myself and disrespecting the girls, the way they were talking and where it was heading. I want more than that.

"You know something? This is the longest in my adult life I've ever been single."

Somewhere between the night on his knees in his room and the Flying Elvi jump in Tampa, something within Brian Balducci had changed.

Someone asked him about it.

"You know what I think?" he said. "Christ gave His life and still gives it. Even though it happened two thousand years ago, it still happens every day. Why it happened back then is answered in the present now. I never realized this before. I thought we all just crawled out of the sea."

Brian is obviously a rough work in the making. He himself would tell you so.

But oh, the progress.

These things he also knows: That there is a God, and that He loves people where they are, even when they don't have it all together. That He loves roustabouts, even if they've given people in the parking lot the finger. That there's *no one* beyond

His grace, even a Flying Elvi who had long since lost his way.

In one of his last scribbled notes before he died in his bathroom, the real Elvis said: "I feel so alone sometimes. The night is quiet for me. I'd love to be able to sleep. I'm glad that everyone is gone now. I'll probably not rest. I have no need for all this. Help me, Lord."[12]

Today, on the road with the Elvi, Brian often lip-synchs some words from "Heartbreak Hotel," perhaps the most auto-biographical of all Elvis songs. His baby's left him, he sings. Well, since my baby left me, I found a new place to dwell. It's down at the end of Lonely Street, at Heartbreak Hotel."

Brian Balducci is not really on Lonely Street. He's met the keeper of his soul.

A Mother's Prayer

Chris's Story

At first light the intersection was empty and still.

Except for remnants of flares on the asphalt, there were few signs of the fearful crash that had occurred five hours before. Now, in this exquisite time of day in the Vegas Valley, the sun stretched its rays from the mountains in the east, across the city and its suburbs, and into the desert to the west.

A few hours earlier, some cops and a representative of the coroner's office had finished their grim work with flashlights at Rainbow Boulevard and Windmill Lane, three and a half miles southwest of the Strip. A demolished car that had flipped over a concrete barricade and landed on its roof had been removed. Now, as light filled the mostly uninhabited desert beyond, all was beautiful and tranquil.

It was a Saturday morning in the last week of July.

At that moment in the pleasure palaces of Vegas, people were sleeping off the night before. Others, with a cigarette in one hand and a rum and Coke in the other, were at the slot machines, trying to beat the odds that return eighty-seven cents on the dollar to the house. Still others were at the marriage license office, open round the clock on weekends, arranging a wedding that day to someone they had met and bedded the night before. The Strip and its environs were beginning to stir. Drinks were already being served at breakfast bars.

But out in the desert all remained still.

By mid-morning a vehicle with a boy and two girls in their mid-to-late teens pulled up at the intersection. They parked near the concrete barricade where the accident had occurred. They carried candles, a bouquet of carnations, and a picture of a young man whose hair was blond. Leaving their gifts on the barrier, they returned to their car, sat inside for awhile, and then drove slowly away.

Soon other young people in cars and SUVs began to appear. They placed more candles on the barrier, and left notes and cards and pictures and poems. Several single red roses were laid atop the wall. Small knots of teens stood by and talked.

The more people arrived, the longer they stayed. In the heat of midafternoon, some young people had been there for hours, and cars were parked along both sides of Rainbow. Some friends strummed guitars and sang songs. Others said prayers in front of what by now had become a shrine.

Early in the afternoon a bank of clouds and a soft, cooling breeze came in. It rained gently and intermittently. And for the remainder of the long day, as word spread from friend to friend among these Sierra Vista High School students, something remarkable happened.

A rainbow appeared above the accident site at Rainbow and Windmill almost every time another group of friends drove up. A cell phone photo someone took at the scene shows that on one occasion there was even a rainbow *within* a rainbow—one shining brightly beneath another.

It almost seemed as if a friend named Chris was sending a message from heaven.

Chris Gunderson had turned eighteen three days before. Now he was sitting alone in front of a supermarket in Henderson, Vegas's mammoth southern suburb.

It was half past midnight and he was trying to reach someone on his cell. He was wearing board shorts, skater shoes, and no shirt. His thick blond hair was dirty and matted and cut bushlike at the ears. His upper body was covered with dust, and there were scratches, cuts, and some blood on his back.

Drew Bodine had been to a late movie with a friend. On his way home alone, he had stopped at the market to pick up milk and orange juice.

As he approached in the dim light of the parking lot, he noticed Chris with a cell in his hand. Their eyes met. For a moment Drew thought he was about to be asked for a cigarette or to buy some alcohol. But neither said a word.

When Drew was going through the checkout, he noticed Chris had come inside and was sitting near the customer service counter. He had come in to use the store's phone. And as he was talking on it, he began to cry and had to brush away tears.

A feeling overcame Drew unlike any other he had experienced.

"I felt a flood of the Holy Spirit just grab my heart," he recalls. "It was as if God was saying: 'Do something about this. This guy needs your help.'

"I saw him hang up the phone and walk out of the store. So just as I was paying, I said a quick prayer: *God, if I'm supposed to do something for this guy, would You let me know what it is when I see him?*"

Chris was sitting slouched against the wall. This time he looked directly at Drew while wiping away tears with the base of his hand.

"Hey, man, you need help?" Drew asked.

Chris's face brightened. "I could use a ride to my house," he said. "Would you mind?"

"No problem," Drew replied. He was thinking, *That's all? Just a lift?*

As they were walking to Drew's truck, Chris suddenly stopped and said, "You know, there's only one thing."

"What's that?"

"I live in Southern Highlands, and that's about twenty minutes from here."

"That's cool, I'll take you," Drew replied.

Southern Highlands is one of Henderson's most luxurious bedroom communities, carved out of the desert. It features villas and a Robert Trent Jones golf course.

Chris, shirtless and with his back cut and scraped and spotted with congealed blood, hopped up into the passenger side of Drew's new truck. The fabric seats were spotless.

Drew was slightly ashamed of his first thought: *Gosh, please don't lean against the cushion. If you get blood on the fabric, how will I get it out?*

"If you live in Southern Highlands," he said, "how did you end up here on foot?

Chris told him the story.

He, his girlfriend, Sara, and another teenage couple had spent the day exploring parts of the Colorado River a number of miles south of Hoover Dam and Lake Mead.

Chris and his friends had stayed along the river until after dark. They had been drinking beer and, although Chris didn't mention it, most likely smoking marijuana. At one point, he and the other guy had hiked away to go skinny-dipping. And when they returned, Chris had found Sara more than a little friendly with a guy she had met while they were gone.

Chris told Drew that the two couples had been on their way back to Vegas about ten or eleven that night when he and Sara got into a heated argument. Intense bickering was not new to them; it characterized their relationship.

The argument on this night erupted when they were heading west through Henderson. Sara pulled her car to the shoulder and kicked Chris out. She threatened to call the police. Not wanting to risk getting arrested, he got out and hiked to the market.

Now, riding with Drew, Chris said he had been calling the police from the store to cover himself—notifying them he had left his girlfriend's car.

It was a lot for Drew to take in.

"By the way, what's your name?" he asked.

"Chris Gunderson. What's yours?"

"Drew. Drew Bodine."

"What do you do around here?" Chris asked.

"I'm a worship leader at a church here. We do a lot of cool stuff. You know, lot's of stuff on the edge, yet all ages. Full band, rock worship team. I think you'd like it."

Chris seemed pensive for a moment. And then, inexplicably, he broke down and started to cry.

"What's wrong?" Drew asked.

"It just reminds me," Chris muttered. "I accepted Christ in my life before. Back when I was fourteen. I used to play drums in a church, just jamming with a guy I'd get together with there during the week. Abilene, Texas. Beltway Park Baptist Church. My mother used to take me there. This guy was the youth pastor and he was cool."

Chris put his hand to his eyes to wipe away tears again.

"It's just hard because I've been so far away," he continued.

"I'm doing so many horrible things. I'm drinking way, way too much, I'm doing drugs, my mouth is terrible. I've kind of lost what I loved. You know, going to church, going there with my mom. She used to say I was God's gift to her.

"But I've been so far away, man. Weed. Ecstasy. Drinking all the time. I drink so much, sometimes I think I'm an alcoholic."

Drew looked over at Chris. "Buddy," he said, "you need to get your life straight."

"I know," Chris replied. "And I really want to."

The conversation got around to his upbringing. His parents separated when he was four. Chris lived with his mom until he was seven. But after his parents were finally divorced and he was about to enter the third grade, his father arrived in Abilene, took him to Disneyland, and never returned, taking him to live in Vegas instead.

Chris's father was a contractor who partied his brains out, bought houses he couldn't afford, and moved from place to place in the valley whenever he went into default.

Chris told Drew he loved his father, an alcoholic, and said his dad needed him to help keep his life straight. But there were times he was so abusive that Chris slept in his own car. Chris had his first taste of alcohol at age ten when he had to clean up the house after one of his dad's parties and experimented by finishing what was left in all the beer cans. His first experience with marijuana came through a bong pipe he shared with his dad at thirteen.

After awhile Chris's mom and dad reached an accommodation that allowed Chris to live with his mom in Abilene each summer during high school. It gave Chris a little stability. And, for the first time in his life, it afforded him the chance to attend a church.

Chris's mom tried to lead him to faith. And one day, he

and the youth pastor were sitting in the back of the latter's pickup after playing roller hockey. The pastor started talking about Christ, about how Chris needed to get real with God.

The pastor said a lot of people go through life without making a decision. People have one life, he said. So the time is right now, right here. Because you never know if you'll have another chance tomorrow.

"So that's when Jesus came into my life," Chris said. "I asked Him in right there. But you can see I didn't really live it.

"When it got time to go back to school, I always came back here. Vegas, man, it just never closes. Whereas in Abilene there's nothing to do—everything closes at ten. Last time when I left, my mom bought me a Bible. In the airport all I was doing was reading it. It was the coolest. And then I came out here and got into alcohol and drugs."

The thought of his mother seemed to energize Chris.

"Hey," he said, "you mind if I call my mom real quick? She will not believe you're giving me a ride home and we're talking about Jesus."

It was 3 a.m. in Abilene.

"Sure, go for it," Drew said.

Within a minute he was listening to Chris's end of the conversation.

"Mom, I've got to tell you something. Do you remember how you told me to always love Jesus?…

"Well, tonight, I wanted nothing more than to end my life. But this guy who picked me up is giving me a ride home. He's a worship leader at a church. This church he's at, it's a lot like yours, Mom…

"Yeah, uh huh…

"Yup, I remember…

"Well, alcohol is part of it…

"You know, marijuana, Ecstasy…

"I know, Mom. And I do. I want to come there and spend some time with you…Yup, get my life straight…and I will.

"Yeah, I know…

"I do, I *want* to change. I *want* to come back to Christ…

"Love you too, Mom… Bye."

Drew and Chris rode for awhile without talking.

Soon Chris asked Drew if he had seen the hit movie *Bruce Almighty*, in which the main character, played by Jim Carrey, assumes the power of God until he realizes he can't handle it anymore.

In the climax, Bruce walks down a street in a rainstorm, looks up to heaven, and rages, "You win! I'm done! I don't want to be God! I want You to decide what's right for me!" He immediately gets hit by a truck and dies, only to be sent back to earth to do God's will.

"Remember that scene where Jim Carrey kind of asks God to take him?" Chris said. "That's what I kind of said today.

"I was standing in the desert on the top of this hill, and I just wanted it all to be over. I was standing the way Jim Carrey was standing in the street, and I'm crying out with my eyes shut, 'God, please, just strike me down and kill me!'"

Chris said he had already had an argument with Sara when he went up the hill. And when he shut his eyes and cried out to God, he lost his balance, slipped, and tumbled down the hill for twenty feet, cutting and scraping his back. It happened only five hours before he and Drew met.

The next afternoon Drew was at his parents' home, packing for a trip to California. He heard the voicemail signal on his cell. Sure enough it was Chris.

"Hey, Drew," the recording said, "it's me, Chris, the guy you gave a ride to last night. I really appreciate you helping me. I prayed last night and I feel a sense of peace with God today. If you ever want to get together again, just give me a call."

Drew reached Chris at a car shop where he worked in the far western end of the valley, about three miles northwest of Southern Highlands. It was desert country where kids raced off-road vehicles. Chris had already become a master mechanic, able to tune an engine quickly and precisely.

Chris was busy that day and couldn't talk for long.

Drew said, "We'll definitely get together. I'd just give all your thanks to God for what's happening. He's got His hand on you. Listen, I'm leaving for California tomorrow and won't be back until the weekend.

"But why don't we get together Sunday night? I'm leading worship at my church that morning and you're welcome to come, but let's at least go get some dinner and hang out that night, okay?"

"Cool," Chris said.

Drew called Chris twice more from California, even apologizing once for bugging him.

"You don't understand, man, you can't bug me," Chris said. "I've never had a friend like you who has cared enough about me to help get my life back on track with God."

When Drew got back to Vegas, he called Chris once more on Friday night from the Desert Passage mall in the Aladdin. It was eleven-thirty, and Chris was at the car shop, putting in a late shift.

"Hey, we still on for Sunday night?" Drew asked.

Chris was as up as Drew ever heard him. "Yeah, I'm really glad you called," he said. "Let's do it."

"Seven o'clock?"

"Seven it is," Chris said. "Just give me a call on Sunday and let me know where you want to meet. I'll be there."

Within an hour of his brief exchange with Drew, Chris received another call that cut him to the quick. Some of his friends have said it was from his dad, who supposedly accused Chris of stealing his weed.

Whatever the case, Chris was emotional and would not be staying with his father in Southern Highlands that night. As he often had when things were uncomfortable at home, he would head instead a few miles east to the house of a guy who worked at the shop.

Chris's friends have said he was drinking lightly and may have been smoking marijuana. Whatever the case, he was overwrought—perhaps angry, perhaps crying—as he drove east on Windmill Lane.

Drew led music for two separate weekend services at Central the following morning. At noon he was in his truck on the way to a brunch with his parents at Lake Las Vegas, a scenic resort community near Lake Mead.

He decided to call Chris on the way. There were a few rings on Chris's cell before a middle-aged male voice answered. It was a voice Drew had never heard.

"Is Chris there?" he asked.

"No, he's dead," the man said. His voice was coarse, flat and hard.

"Seriously," Drew said, "can I speak to Chris?"

"No, he's dead!" The man's voice was louder now and edgy.

"Uhh, okay, you've got to stop playing around," Drew said. "I don't know Chris that well. I just met him, and I'd like to speak to Chris, please."

"Are you kidding with me?" the man yelled. "Chris is dead!" And the guy hung up.

"I didn't want to believe what he was saying," Drew recalls. "I called back and said, 'My name's Drew. I'm a worship leader at a church in Henderson. I met Chris the other night and gave him a ride home, and we had plans to go to dinner tonight. And I would like to speak to him if I could."

"I'm his father," Matt Gunderson said. "And I'm telling you that my son is dead. He died in a car accident at the corner of Rainbow and Windmill early yesterday morning around 1 a.m. And if you don't believe me you can go to the accident site and see where his car ran into the wall."

Drew was having trouble with his emotions when he got to Lake Las Vegas. He called both the police and the Clark County coroner's office and confirmed that Chris had been killed.

He knew this had to be God's will, but it was hard to take. And he was certainly wondering why.

The police report of Chris Gunderson's accident is clinical. He was driving an old four-door Subaru Legacy on Windmill Lane, toward the city. It was seventy-eight degrees and the night sky was clear. He was traveling fifty-two miles an hour in a thirty-five-mile-per-hour zone. And he was not wearing a seat belt.

Although new housing communities fill the area today, rare was the car that traveled on Windmill near Rainbow during post-midnight hours back then. You could stand at the intersection for fifteen minutes without seeing a car. The road was straight and flat, and few drivers paid attention to the speed limit.

Speeding into the intersection, Chris apparently saw that three-foot-high concrete barriers totally walled off the extension of Windmill on the other side.

It was too late. There was quite a bit of construction sand atop the roadway, and he skidded through the intersection for one hundred feet. He hit the wall with such force that one of the barriers was pushed backward and broken in two. Chris's car flipped over the barriers and landed on its roof. He almost certainly died instantly.

About twenty minutes later, Eric Sommer, a friend of Chris's from the shop, happened upon the scene and realized something was amiss. In the glare of his headlights, he went beyond the abutments, saw the overturned car, and discovered the body.

Officers and medical personnel arrived in seven minutes. There was nothing they could do. Around 4 a.m., some three and a half hours after the accident, rescuers used the "Jaws of Life" to cut away the driver's door and extract Chris's body.

In a stranger-than-fiction coincidence, one of Chris's friends from the shop—the very friend to whose home he was headed—turned out to be the tow-trucker the police called to haul away the car. Chris died just two blocks from this friend's house.

On Monday Drew knew he had to talk to Chris's mother in Abilene and tell her that God had been working in her son's life. The only name he remembered from what Chris had told him was Beltway. So he punched into his laptop the words "Beltway Abilene Texas" and up popped the name of the church.

Within minutes Drew was on the phone with the receptionist, asking if she knew of a single mother who went to the church and had just lost a son named Chris. The receptionist said she didn't. But fifteen minutes later she called back with the name of Chris Gunderson's mother: Monica Koch.

Fifteen minutes later Drew was on the phone with Chris's mom. She is twice divorced, lives with her mother and daughter, a year younger than Chris, and works as an ad saleswoman. She has not had an easy life.

"Ma'am," he said, "my name is Drew Bodine, and I'm the worship leader at the church in Henderson, Nevada, who picked up Chris last week and helped him get home."

She was speechless. She told him she and her mother had been praying that if Chris were in heaven, this friend of his named Drew would find a way to call.

"I'm calling to tell you that Chris recommitted his life to Christ the week before he died," Drew said.

"It was everything I prayed for," Monica says. "When Chris told me that the man who picked him up lived on a street named Glistening Cloud Drive in Henderson, I told him he must be an angel."

In a sense, it was a confirmation for Monica. "Beneath it all he always had a calmness and a sweet spirit," she says today of her son. "A parent just knows when a child is supposed to be God's and has that spirit in him."

She remembers the last days they were together when he visited over the previous Christmas. He was surrounded shoulder-high by gifts so you could hardly see his head.

It was a tender moment for her because, when the presents were opened, he came to her and said, "You know, Mom, you didn't have to do this."

Monica has vivid memories of her son's last days and the

aftermath of his death. In fact, Chris was speaking to her on his cell when Drew first saw him slouched outside the supermarket. He was telling her about crying out to God on the hill in the desert only hours before, beseeching Him to end his life because of all the pain.

"It sent a chill down my spine when he told me that," she recalls. "I remember thinking, *Don't ever yell at God and ask Him to take your life, because He most certainly can.*"

On Sunday, the day after Monica learned of Chris's death in a phone call from her son's father, she grieved for hours. Then late in the day, just to get her mind off everything, she went outside and cut her lawn.

As she mowed, she said, "God, why did You have to take him now, just when he's recommitted his life to You? It would've been so wonderful to have known my son when he was saved because he had such a good heart even when he wasn't."

According to Monica, God spoke to her very plainly.

Did you not tell Me I could have him? He said to her heart.

"You see," Monica says, "on the day before Chris died, I actually said to a couple of ladies at work, 'I've turned my son over to God, and He'll do with him whatever He wants as long as his soul belongs to Him.'"

Then God said something else to Monica.

Besides, He told her, *was Christopher not dead when I gave him to you? And didn't I give him to you for a little while?*

Monica explains that Chris nearly died at birth. He was born on her eighteenth birthday—their birthdays will be forever the same. And when he was born, the umbilical cord, wrapped three times around his neck, was choking him. She recalls that for the longest time and through all the emergency procedures, she never heard him cry.

She remembers yelling, even demanding, "God, give me

my baby!" And only then did Chris's crying begin.

"During his early years I would just hold him and we used to sing that gentle hymn that goes, 'Jesus…Jesus…There's just something about that name.' He would ask me to sing that to him over and over until he fell asleep. So God told me He gave him to me for awhile.

"Who am I to argue?"

Chris Gunderson was laid to rest in Abilene five days after he died.

There was a memorial service at Beltway Park at which Rick Blackington, the youth pastor who led Chris to Christ, and Drew, the friend who reconnected him, each spoke. Drew had composed a song for Chris, "In Need of Faith," and he sang it there. The second chorus goes:

> I know I have faith
> That you're living life that leads to no more harm.
> Yeah, you're living in God's arms.
> I know I have faith
> That you've been forgiven and He has washed you new
> Because He's loving and true
> And He gave me you.

There was a second service at a park near Sierra Vista High School, where Chris would have become a senior six weeks later. Drew sang there as well.

Afterward, there was curiosity among Chris's friends about who Drew was. Word had made the rounds. Chris had been talking about his faith and his new friend and how his life was going to change.

Drew says:

"One guy told me that on Friday night, the last night of his life, Chris had some alcohol to drink. But he said: 'This is it, this is the last time. I'm laying drugs down, I'm laying alcohol down, I'm getting my life straight this weekend.'

"I believe that night was when he totally surrendered to God."

In fact, within an hour of Chris's last talk with Drew, Chris was wrapped in the arms of the Almighty.

CHAPTER EIGHT

Reimagine You

I sat next to Chris Gunderson's mom, Monica, and wept. Chris had so much life ahead of him and died just as he was working things out. Monica had joined us near the one-year anniversary of Chris's death. In our services I shared her story and the importance Drew played in Chris's life, then Drew performed the song he wrote and presented her with flowers. That was when it hit me—God had brought me down a winding road not unlike both Chris and *American Idol* hopeful Jason Walters. A road I once thought I'd gone too far down to ever make it back.

I grew up a long way from Vegas, both culturally and geographically, in Amarillo, Texas. Yet my story uniquely prepared me for life and faith in this city of second chances. I'm the youngest of four. My dad was a World War II vet who came from humble beginnings. An entrepreneur and businessman, he started and grew a successful commercial refrigeration business. Mom helped him at the office and managed the house. My family was down to earth, practical, loving, and stable. Church attendance was mandatory, and Sunday lunch at our home was a huge family gathering with food, laughter, and an occasional all-day Monopoly game.

I was an impatient kid, always into something and unable to be still. I guess that's why I found our all-American family more restricting than satisfying, and I went looking for something completely different. The first time I smoked pot was in junior high. It was lunch break and I, along with several friends, huddled up at the corner of the school building and passed a joint around. Initially pot gave me bragging rights and added to my "cool" factor among friends. I was mature, older. At least that was what I thought at fourteen. I had always been somewhat out of step in school, never quite fitting in. The drugs helped me to feel better about myself and about life in general. Soon I was using pot every day, and then progressing on to anything and everything I could get my hands on—cocaine, methamphetamines, LSD, Ecstasy, you name it.

Through all of this I continued to function, but I had developed an addiction I couldn't seem to shake. I quickly progressed from bragging to keeping secrets. Addiction is incredibly isolating. You begin to drink or use drugs, and you notice how it loosens you up, and you become the life of the party. But soon enough you are hiding with your addiction, alone in the back room, feeling completely numb to everything.

One night, after four years of abuse, I sensed I was at a crossroads, that if something didn't change I would be sucked into the black hole of addiction forever. I felt afraid and weary. Falling to my knees, way out of my comfort zone, I asked for help. As I prayed to God, I half expected the walls of our house to collapse! I know it's a cliché—another drug addict finds God—but for me it was the defining moment of my life. My parents were people of faith, so I had a sense of what I needed to do. I began to pray daily, to read my Bible, and to distance myself from the parties and the people I had surrounded myself with. I quit drugs cold turkey and never went back.

The last four years of my life felt like a nightmare I had just woken up from, except in reality I had done a lot of damage to people I loved, and it would take years to rebuild my life. I still remember so clearly my arduous climb to sobriety, every day having to fight my desire for another high. Drugs should have killed me, and they almost did. I never could have made it back without God and His grace.

Though I've been clean now for eighteen years, I'll never forget what it is to be made powerless by an addiction. I know how it feels to be broken, to feel trapped to the point of hopelessness, to be numb to everything and ready to give up. Out of this experience comes my tremendous compassion for others who are struggling, and I believe this is part of why I ended up in Las Vegas. They say it takes one to know one, and in my case the misery I experienced coming out of addiction allows me to relate to people going through all kinds of pain in their lives.

What floored me as I sat next to Monica was how God's grace can reach out to us at many points in our journey, even our final moments. His grace changes everything in our lives. It was transforming Chris in the days before he died, as if God were preparing both him and his mother. When we've done so many things wrong, we need God's help to believe our lives can ever be made right again. That help can come anytime, anywhere; it's just waiting for us to be ready to receive it. And when we do, God's grace changes how we see our past, present, and future. It changes how we see ourselves.

For years my past addiction significantly damaged my self-image. No matter how much I achieved or what I accomplished after God put my life back together, it was not good enough.

I felt I would never match up, never be whole.

Did you know that all of the chemical, mineral, and skin elements that make up the average human body are only worth about $4.50? I often felt like I was worth about $4.50. Sometimes I still do. One of our greatest struggles is self-hatred (and a lot of times we've made mistakes in our lives that seem to prove our point). We hear voices from the past and the present saying: "You're no good." "You'll never amount to anything." "You are so ugly." "You don't matter." We bear a heavy load of guilt and failure that drags down our view of ourselves.

After becoming a Christian, I spent several years wrestling with forgiveness, trying to remove all those negative voices from my head. I could forgive others, I could even believe that God had forgiven me, but I could not forgive myself. One day I heard someone teach from this passage: "This is love: not that we loved God, but that he loved us and sent his Son as an atoning sacrifice for our sins" (1 John 4:10). Afterward I hurried out and went to a quiet place. As I reflected on God's amazing love, it finally sunk in that the primary thing was not my love for God or my love for myself. The primary thing was and is *God's love for me*. What *God* thinks of me matters infinitely more than what *I* think of me. That is what defines the greatest love of all. And from that love I respond to God as one deeply flawed, yet unconditionally loved.

The Bible teaches that we are all created in the image of God. This knowledge is where our worth begins, but we often take it for granted, not realizing the power in this truth. As I studied the Bible, I was surprised by how radical this message was in its ancient context. The Hebrews who first received the message knew what it meant to feel lost and confused about who they were. For forty years they roamed the wilderness while headed to the Promised Land. They had been slaves for generations before this, and that was still a powerful force in how they viewed themselves. It was to this group of ex-slaves that God revealed the first five books of the Bible—and the story of His loving creation of humankind—through Moses.

We can hardly grasp the mind-blowing nature of the claim that *everyone* is made in the image of God. In the ancient Near East, people were seen as an afterthought, created primarily to serve the needs of the gods. The gods' main need was food, and people were expected to provide for this need. Only kings were said to be in the image and likeness of the gods. Everyday people such as shepherds, farmers, and construction workers were merely human, slaves to the gods.

Understanding this opened my eyes to why the book of Genesis emphasizes God's unique creation of humans: "So God *created* man *in his own image*, *in the image of God* he *created* him; male and female he *created* them" (Genesis 1:27). Three times in one verse it states God "created" and twice it emphasizes "in his image." This pattern is virtually repeated in Genesis 5:1 and the following verses. How can we so easily dismiss ourselves and deny our value when God has been screaming for thousands of years that we all matter?

The image of God points to the elements within us that reflect His character, glory, and goodness. It means we have the ability to think, love, and make moral choices. He's created us with His unique stamp on our lives, and He will provide for our needs. We are not simply slaves! We are royalty, sons and daughters of the King! God's image gives us worth precisely because of His greatness, not ours. He is the One who is worthy, and it is His image—and His worthiness—we bear.

When I realized the value I have in God's eyes, it changed me. I began to reimagine myself as one loved deeply by God, irrespective of what I felt. I am loved before, during, and after my sin. I am loved when I feel unworthy. I am loved in spite of myself. I wanted approval from others to validate my worth, I wanted to show everyone I could make something of myself, I wanted to become someone. But that day I realized I would never find what I searched for because I already had it. I had to personally embrace God's grace in a life-transforming way.

Bono, lead singer of U2, captured the radical nature of God's grace when he said:

> It's a mind-blowing concept that the God who created the universe might be looking for company, a real relationship with people, but the thing that keeps me on my knees is the difference between grace and karma.... Grace defies reason and logic. Love interrupts, if you like, the consequences of your actions, which in my case is very good news indeed, because I've done a lot of stupid stuff.... I'd be in big trouble if karma was going to finally be my judge.... It doesn't excuse my mistakes, but I'm holding out for grace. I'm holding out that Jesus took my sins onto the cross, because I know who I am, and I hope I don't have to depend on my own religiosity.[13]

I'm holding out for grace as well.

Grace offers us relief from the crushing weight of the past. And this frees us to hope for a better future. One weekend at Central we had a dozen people write a few words of what God had done in their lives on pieces of old cardboard. One person took a piece of paper and did her own reimagining. She dropped it off at the front desk on her way out (see image). On the paper she described her present with terms like "loneliness, broke, prostitute, kleptomaniac, angry, bitter..." What moved me was how she envisioned her future: "Healthy, wealthy, whole in spirit, married with four children."

Was she just pie-in-the-sky dreaming? No. God's grace can truly change a future. He can heal and work and transform a person in the most profound way. There is hope for her and for all of us because of Him.

Yet this grace is not for the faint of heart. This is not feel-good-about-yourself psychobabble. This is real, hard work. Living in this grace, reimagining yourself, requires dealing with sin in your life, confessing that sin, and coming clean before God and others. Bearing God's image is a serious responsibility.

In the ancient Near East, kings would set up an image of themselves in the distant parts of their territory. The image of the king would establish authority and dominion even in the king's absence. In Genesis God creates man in His image and empowers him to be His royal representative on the earth. Our responsibility is to bear God's image well.

Next time you are tempted to yell at your kids, shade the truth, cheat, or let your temper go...remember, you are not only made in the image of God, you are made to *bear* that image. You will fail (we all do), but God's forgiveness will allow you to start anew and be His representative to all you meet. Through serving, using your gifts, standing up for the poor and oppressed, through mercy and defending those who need to be defended, you bear God's image in the world.

Living in Vegas I've learned that God is in the business of setting people free. I'm reminded of the Israelites who lived so long in slavery. In His grace and mercy, God made a way for them to be brought back from the land of captivity. Here is how one of them described the experience: "When the LORD brought back the captives to Zion, we were like men who dreamed. Our mouths were filled with laughter, our tongues with songs of joy. Then it was said among the nations, 'The LORD has done great things for them.' The LORD has done great things for us, and we are filled with joy" (Psalm 126:1–3).

When God delivered them, they were like people who dreamed again. Not only that, but also their mouths were filled with laughter and their tongues with songs of joy. A whole new future had opened up to them. You may feel captive to many things today—a relationship that seems lifeless, a job that no longer brings you joy, an addiction you can't seem to kick. You may feel trapped under financial or family pressure, but God can give you the ability to reimagine your life and dream again. When we surrender our lives to God in faith, He begins to lead us out of our captivity.

Tom found this freedom after he was touched by an experience at Central. Participants in a gathering at church were asked, while holding a small rock, to think of the sins they had committed and the burdens they carried. Then they were asked to leave the rock at the door as they left. This was a picture of forgiveness in their lives. A few days later, Tom called the church. He explained that he liked the rock thing, but the rock wasn't big enough for his sins. So he went and found the biggest boulder he could lift and put it in the back of his truck. Then he took spray paint and painted everything he had ever done wrong all over the rock. As if this was not enough, he then drove out to Hoover Dam, about a half-hour from Vegas, at three o'clock in the morning and, as he tells it, heaved the boulder over the dam! He called to explain how great it felt to get that off his chest...or out of his truck! I wouldn't recommend throwing boulders over your local dam, but it does remind us that "as far as the east is from the west, so far has he removed our transgressions from us" (Psalm 103:12).

What kind of rock is weighing you down? What sorts of words or deeds are painted on it? Maybe it is time to toss it out of your life and experience the freedom God offers.

PART THREE:
GRACE TO BELONG

Wheel of Fortune

Geoff's Story

It matters not where you move in the Vegas Valley, they are always there, forever warbling their inimitable sound. Slot machines—nickel slots, dollar slots, progressive slots. Slot machines in the supermarkets, slots in the 7-Elevens, slots in the local casinos on Boulder Highway, slots on the game floors of the Bellagio and Caesars and Wynn Las Vegas and the Luxor.

Silver-haired ladies putting bill after bill in the machine with their right hand and smoking with their left. Cocktail waitresses in their dance-girl suits forever taking drink orders. Total anonymity—men and women whiling away the hours, looking for the spinning reel on the video screen to make them wealthy, half-sitting on their seats, a few with oxygen canisters on the floor beside them.

But oh, the romance of it! The sounds of the environment—over on the other side somebody else's slot has just boomed "WHEEL!...OF!...FORTUNE!!"

With the slots, impersonality reigns. There's no revealing how little you know, as can happen at the blackjack table. No one stares you down, never blinking, never revealing, waiting for you to fold. With the slots, the game always comes to you, at your speed and on your time.

There they are, sitting at their individual screens, hitting the button with a flick of their index finger, spending a few more credits for another spin of the reels. *Maybe they'll line up this time.* Little do they know that all across the valley two-thirds of the house's revenue comes from the slots. From slots, of all places—not from craps, not from the tables.

It's the geniuses in the back rooms who know the probabilities. It's the masterminds in silk suits who pay out enough to entice more spending, linking up vast networks of slots that produce Megabucks payoffs. While slots players blindly pump in more cash, these businessmen skim huge profits, building slot empires that trade on the New York Stock Exchange.

In 1997 Geoff Sage was at the top of his game, working as the chief financial officer of one of the most powerful slot machine companies in the United States. He was one of the quintessential backroom Las Vegans—one of the geniuses who made money off the odds. And if you had told him that God would someday use his lightning-quick mind, his way with big bucks, and his penchant for strategizing to help lead the biggest church in Vegas, he would have told you that the odds were higher than 100,000,000 to 1.

Geoff is the only child of a Jewish loan shark and a chain-smoking Italian-American mother. His parents separated after he was born, his father staying in the Bronx with Geoff while his mother moved to Miami Beach. One day after leaving his second grade class, two women Geoff didn't recognize showed up and spirited him away to Florida. One was his mom and the other his aunt. From then until high school he was literally kidnapped now and then from either parent's custody. Finally, when his mother moved to Vegas to work as a casino restaurant hostess, teenaged Geoff followed her there.

He learned to love the city but not his heavily perfumed, chain-smoking mom. His was a calculated life in which emotions were submerged. It was all about the numbers. He knew about margins and profits and the balancing of books long before his time. He saw his first slot at Circus Circus, but he was never a big-time player.

But that's not to say he wasn't interested in the business of gambling.

In Florida, his pals had bet the undefeated Dolphins in their glory days and usually won. Though a big Dolphins fan himself, he often bet against them when he moved to Vegas. For him the game was not about loyalty, but the steady accumulation of money. Besides, he soon was a jack-of-all-trades (tending bar, bussing tables) at Jubilation, a disco between Harmon and the Strip, taking home up to $350 a night, so he could afford to gamble a little.

Geoff's interest in money led him to a business degree at University of Nevada Las Vegas, and when he graduated, he joined a public accounting firm. He was a tall, dark-haired, and quiet guy who was extremely good with numbers and ledgers. If you had been at Caesars or Wayne Newton's Aladdin before midnight on New Year's Eve, you might have found him holed up in the cashier's cage as the revelry on the floor mounted. He didn't care about revelry. He was quietly counting the chips and markers before the clock struck midnight.

Geoff was eventually given the chance to become controller of Aspen Creek Gaming, a small Vegas company that owned a couple of casinos in Colorado and was increasing its share of the slot-machine business in Nevada. Aspen Creek's owner, Gus Stanos, offered Geoff $55,000 with no raises, take it or leave it. But Stanos said he would get bonuses from future profits—if there were any.

Geoff jumped at it. He and his wife, Brenda, a nurse in the trauma unit of Vegas's biggest hospital, had started to raise a family and certainly could use the money. His new position made him responsible for all of the company's accounts and internal audits. It proved to be a shrewd move for both him and Stanos.

Stanos was one of the founding fathers of video poker and an innovator of modern slots. He was headstrong and mercurial. But he knew the slot business as well or better than anyone in the country—knew what made the players tick, where the game was headed with computers, where the power was shifting between the casinos and slot geniuses like himself. Geoff, who would become the chief financial officer of Aspen Creek, kept the company on course.

The video revolution was rapidly transforming the gambling business. Millions of new players were being lured into the casinos. They played video poker not against the house, as at the craps table, but against a pay table for various hands that was posted on the game machine. Many of the machines would eventually be named after TV shows—*The Price Is Right*, *Saturday Night Live*, *M*A*S*H*, *Gilligan's Island*.

It used to be that every slot looked like a shiny little warehouse of iron. But now the most popular slots were becoming part of a more extensive casino environment. Whole slot sections of a casino floor were being themed to entertain the player—if the slot had a jungle theme, so did the immediate surroundings on the floor. Suddenly there were animal sounds coming from hidden speakers, spooky rain forest noises as players decided whether to increase their bets.

Stanos understood that there were two kinds of players in slots or video poker. The first was the savvy player. This guy or this woman knew which machines gave them the most credits for a full house, and where to find the machine with the biggest payback.

But Stanos also knew that with the other type of player it was simply about excitement and entertainment. You would always have the savvy player with you. But the number of those who played for excitement and fun now seemed to be rocketing—it was an upside in the market that dazzled the eyes of the visionaries.

It was all about how to make losing fun.

The slot guy who wanted excitement and entertainment didn't really sit down with the expectation of winning, Stanos realized. For him, the odds weren't really the point. This player sat down with the expectation of having a blast.

Stanos, and by extension Geoff, were discovering the modern secret of slots.

"It's all about having somebody walk away having lost their money, but having enjoyed the experience," Geoff says.

"It's making a losing experience a winning experience. The slot machines we were producing did that."

As for Geoff, he was riding the tide. The higher he went at Aspen Creek and the more people who joined the company, the better his hours became. He was now making *strategic* decisions. There were underlings outside his office doors. He came and went as he pleased, was home at a reasonable hour, played sports with his two young boys, and lived what he considered the all-American life.

Meanwhile, Aspen Creek kept the revenue rolling in by continuing to conduct its business outside the box. Aspen Creek was the first slot vendor to say to the casinos, "No, we're not going to sell you our slot machine for $5,000. We're going to let you use it in return for a share of the upside."

"We didn't sell our games—we essentially rented them," Geoff says. "This is kind of an in-your-face way of doing business, but it's how we operated. Say you're the casino owner. As long as the games did well for you after thirty, sixty, or ninety days, they justified the idea of you paying a recurring revenue stream back to us. And the slot manager knew if they didn't do well, we'd come and take them out."

This was Gus Stanos's business model.

It was brilliant.

Needing to upgrade and modernize their slot floors, many casinos were facing mammoth cash outlays. Stanos knew this, of course. He pushed the idea of the casinos becoming partners with him. Buy his new, more entertaining slots at no initial cost, he suggested. Then they would turn a profit while furnishing Aspen Creek a fixed percentage of the revenue stream.

It was a win-win for everybody.

Aspen Creek's rise on the strength of its aggressive marketing and game development made it well-known in the gaming industry almost overnight.

Stanos, always thinking, always staying two steps ahead, bought Worldwide Game Distributors, a company that shared his vision for upping the slots' entertainment ante to generate more profits. The consolidated company soon produced its own trademarked games for the casinos.

Meanwhile, Geoff was reaping his reward, his salary climbing ever higher. The day was at hand, though, when his time would no longer be his own. He had to tell Brenda he could no longer mind the boys while she was working trauma. She became a stay-at-home mom, and he became a stay-longer-at-the-office dad. The trajectory of the company was amazing him. Who would have thought it?

Aspen Creek took a risk and became a publicly traded

company, a move that brought in a mountain of cash, which Stanos and his new partners used to create the next generation of slot games. One of these games, dreamed up by Stanos and Aspen Creek's new chief operating officer, P. J. Riccardi, had a big, multicolored, carnival-like wheel that sat above the machine. It was divided into twenty-two pie-like sections labeled with dollar amounts from $25 to $1,000.

When the reels lined up and the "bonus" logo appeared, the player would push a button and the wheel would spin. The player felt a rush that no other game could give him. Once the wheel spun he never came out a loser.

The odds, however, were much greater than 22-1 that the player would win the $1,000. Because of the computer programming and the geniuses in the back room, they were more like 999-1.

Aspen Creek's wheel first appeared on a slot machine called Wheel of Gold. It was very successful. But International Game Technology, a titan in the slots business, held a license to invent a slot named Wheel of Fortune, after the TV game show. Light bulbs went off in executives' minds. The two companies struck a deal, the sound bite from the TV show was added, and soon casinos all over Vegas were echoing the recorded cries of "WHEEL!...OF!...FORTUNE!!"

Slot players went nuts.

By the late nineties, Aspen Creek's stock had climbed from $12 a share to $60—a breathtaking run-up that reflected the strength of the market at the time and Aspen Creek's strong position in the gaming industry. Everybody benefited, not least of all Geoff. And so far he wasn't paying a price for his supersonic ride.

Late that year Stanos decided to make another public offering—1.8 million shares that were held by his family at $91. By now Geoff had been functioning as chief financial officer of Aspen Creek. And as part of his responsibility, he was asked to join Stanos and Riccardi in public appearances before groups of potential investors in major cities around the country.

For some executives, the trappings of such high-power "road shows"—private corporate jets from city to city, limousines waiting at the airport with their motors running, five-star hotels, meetings in corporate suites with august views of New York Harbor, the Boston Commons, or San Francisco Bay—would be the ultimate fruits of success.

But not for Geoff.

He had a secret no one at Aspen Creek imagined. He suffered from severe anxiety whenever he had to deliver a talk in public. The road show merely made his insecurity that much worse. It was like facing a five-hundred-pound gorilla.

Before the October tour began, Geoff took a series of intense public speaking classes. On some sections of the weeklong tour, Brenda, her father, and of course Stanos accompanied him.

Despite all his stage fright, Geoff proved to be something of a hit. He may have been sweating bullets up at the podium, he may have been on the verge of panic attacks, but his listeners never knew it. Investors snapped up Aspen Creek's stock at the level required.

Unknown to Geoff or Riccardi, however, a battle was being waged in Stanos's mind. He lost a lot of control when the company went public, and now he wanted out. It fell to Geoff and Riccardi to find a way for him to leave and still salvage the value of his company.

On the heels of the last stock offering, this latest imperative placed an enormous amount of additional pressure on Geoff and Riccardi.

The plan they ultimately devised was to buy out the Stanos family while at the same time recapitalizing the company yet again. Where would the staggering amount of cash required come from? The only way to raise it was to stage an elaborate three-week road show—the mother of all road shows in their minds—with Geoff taking the lead as the chief financial spokesman.

"Talk about stress," Geoff recalls. "I immediately became a walking basket case."

But Geoff found some comfort in a message he heard at Central one Sunday. Shortly before the road show opened, one of the messages happened to be about managing stress in the workplace. The timing—God's timing—couldn't have been better.

Earlier in their marriage Geoff and Brenda tried a number of churches and synagogues but didn't find themselves comfortable at any. For all intents and purposes they were indifferent to religion. But some ten years earlier, Stanos had introduced Geoff to Central, then a midsized but rapidly growing church he happened to be attending in Vegas. Geoff, Brenda, and their two sons had kept going each Sunday while Stanos eventually fell away.

Geoff, a nonobservant Jew, and Brenda, a nonpracticing Catholic, were not interested in joining or professing a belief in Christ. On the contrary, they held an annual Passover Seder at home to maintain at least some Jewish tradition for their sons. But they did find the pastor's messages practical and found some of his advice useful.

"I had an uncanny ability to filter what I was hearing, taking the pieces that applied to my life and hearing those," he says. "But when a message talked about Christ, I had a way of just shutting it off and not hearing it. The Bible talks about the fact that when we seek Him we'll find Him. But if we're not seeking, it's hard to find Him."

Thankfully, Geoff's filter let the message about stress in the workplace sink in. The primary point was that Christ doesn't want people to carry the baggage of stress and anxiety at home or at work. When Christ died on the cross for each of us, He allowed us to place our burdens at the foot of His cross. He was ready and willing to take fear and anxiety off people's shoulders.

What a novel idea, Geoff thought.

He had close to one hundred meetings scheduled. He had the right training and the requisite experience, but he was transfixed by how high the stakes were and by his anxiety before groups or crowds. In some ways he was dreading it.

"I was dealing with a fear that a lot of people know very well," he says. "I had a tendency to opt out of speaking whenever I could. But it was a paradox. I learned that only by confronting the fear would I get better.

"The faith part of it for me was the revelation that this [stress and fear] isn't what God wants for us. He's a willing participant in these things."

No matter the city they were in—New York, Chicago, San Francisco—the days were the same. They started with a six-thirty breakfast meeting with eight to twenty principals from their underwriting investors, Bank of America and Wasserstein Perella.

Lunches were one-on-ones with a single investor or with four, or with groups of eight, fifteen, or a hundred. Bankers, Geoff found, are sensitive to room size. They lead you around, service you, show you their power views from the 52nd floor overlooking the harbor. But you make your presentation and answer their questions with *your back to the view*. They are the ones who enjoy the majesty of the harbor.

The private jets and limos came in handy as city-hopping occurred throughout some days. There were meetings on the hour and jets shuttling from place to place. Breakfast in Cincy, mid-morning brunch in Milwaukee, lunch in Chicago, never really eating, always talking, always weighing the stakes, ending the day in Manhattan where three more investment houses were added to the schedule on ten minutes' notice.

Because of the incredibly long days, Geoff resorted to running in the middle of the night to maintain his calm. No matter what time he went to bed, he got up at three in the morning, was in the shower after four, and preparing for the day's business sessions by five.

During the road show, Geoff and Riccardi had a possible end game for Aspen Creek in mind. With the phenomenal growth of the company and the Wheel of Fortune partnership with International Game Technology, it was becoming increasingly clear that a merger or takeover by IGT might someday occur.

IGT was the largest gaming equipment manufacturer in the world. The two companies were so closely aligned that some kind of merger seemed inevitable. Although no one was talking openly about it, there was speculation in the investment community.

But if that merger was ever to occur, this public offering had to be large enough to facilitate that eventual transaction and provide golden parachutes for Geoff and other principals on the Aspen Creek side. After all, Geoff for one would be out of a job if Aspen Creek was taken over by IGT.

This elephant in the room added yet another level of anxiety.

Geoff would be out? Yeah, with a hefty payment, but what would he do? Once the tour began, he prayed to Christ for the first time—before, during, and after every meeting. A Jew praying to a Jewish messiah. He prayed that Christ would remove his stress and anxiety and allow him to speak freely about the offering, without fear.

At what point did Geoff realize that God was carrying him? After all, he was a bundle of nerves before every talk—yet he seemed to be surviving.

"It was more of a process," he recalls. "It was never easy, but as I went through it, I kind of released myself to Him."

There were days when Geoff found himself in a meeting room in Boston with twenty investors before him and four thousand people across the country listening via conference call. All to raise a quarter of a billion dollars. And what were the stakes? That they could lose everything if the market tumbled or even collapsed before the closing date. That the interest just wouldn't be there. That Geoff could fail miserably, forcing him, Riccardi, and the underwriters to redo the offering for significantly less.

That Stanos, ever the cowboy, would call them on the plane in mid-flight and change his mind, telling them he was no longer selling the company and to come back home.

As the future became more uncertain, Geoff found himself leaning on God more and more. The rough road made his faith grow.

On his return to Vegas, Geoff sought out a pastor at Central to talk about the effect the message on stress in the workplace had on him. It had been so important, he had to acknowledge it.

"I knew in my heart that things were going really well for me in my life," he recalls. "There were three reasons I could see. First, I must be very good at what I was doing. Second, I must be in the right place at the right time. Third, God must have a hand on my life. I finally came to the conclusion that my success wasn't due to me or to timing, but to God."

Geoff talked about this new awareness with the pastor.

Afterward, the pastor said, "Well, are you ready to ask Christ into your heart?"

"The way my mind worked, I didn't have any reason to say no," Geoff recalls.

"I guess so," he stammered. "But what do I do?"

The pastor walked around his desk and sat down beside Geoff. He led him in a short prayer, and Geoff found himself asking Christ to fully come into his life as his personal Lord and Savior. He found it incredibly easy and natural.

"When I walked out of his office, I went down an empty corridor and asked myself, *What just happened in there?*

"I knew I had crossed the line of faith. I knew I had done something that I had chosen conscientiously not to do for years. But really knowing about the transaction that had occurred? I'm not sure I knew."

What he did realize was that Central was now more than ever his home.

It was a place where he felt comfortable, never out of place. The members had diverse backgrounds, checkered pasts, and jobs that might be frowned on in some other "religious" circles—but none of that disqualified them from being part of God's family.

Things continued to go well for Geoff at work, as well as for Aspen Creek. Since that day he gave his life to Christ, he has been able to deliver talks before crowds at a much higher level than before. "Not always stress free—on occasion I get reminded of how it used to be," he admits. "But if I speak today in front of a group, I still pray the same prayers, get up there, and do it for His glory, and He just releases me."

The following spring while he was attending a *Forbes* magazine meeting for financial officers in Santa Barbara, California, he went on a five-mile walk from the hotel to the Pacific. About halfway through he felt a sudden urge to stop. Something was tugging at his heart and a near-audible voice was speaking inside him.

He believes the voice was from the Holy Spirit—Christ's very presence living in him.

"He said two things to me," Geoff remembers. "First, go and visit your dad as soon as possible. Second, if IGT comes calling to buy the company, support the transaction and don't worry about your future."

When Geoff got back to Vegas, he booked a flight to Florida to see his father. Without his realizing it, his dad's health had taken a permanent turn for the worse. While in Florida, Geoff quickly got him into a nursing home. He also was able to tell him about the spiritual change in his life. His father died a few months later.

The week after his walk in Santa Barbara, IGT called and began what ultimately became more than a billion-dollar buy-out of Aspen Creek. Stanos, today a quasi-philanthropist who's had a horse in the Kentucky Derby, was not upset to be done with the business for his $350 million cut. P .J. Riccardi went on to become the hugely powerful chief executive of IGT—a titan in his own right. Geoff, handsomely compensated, would be out on his own. It was an odd feeling—like riding a train to nowhere.

For much of that year Geoff worked diligently on the sale

of Aspen Creek. *Lord, my life is not mine—it's Yours,*" he prayed. "*I have You to thank for the success in my life. Use me any way You see fit. Mold me to be the person You want me to be. Thank You, Lord, for my wife and two sons. Thank You for what You've done in my life, what You're now doing, and for what You've yet to do. Just show me the way and I will follow.*"

Early in the merger process he had made a list of things he was going to do if and when he found himself out of work. A fitness freak, marathoner, and long-distance bicyclist, he was going to hire a personal trainer, buy a new mountain bike, and volunteer at Central.

One day, he woke up and decided his list was totally lame—he wanted to make bigger, better plans. So he called the church for another appointment with the pastor. Interestingly, Geoff had decided he could do more at Central than volunteer. Periodically stretched, growing by leaps and bounds, Central had a need for an experienced financial manager without Geoff's realizing it. He and the church's administrator began talking. Today Geoff is the church's treasurer and chief operating officer.

Schooled partly in the casino cages, a former slots guru with a Strip pedigree, he has brought a tremendous level of competency to the financial operations of an organization nobody would have guessed—a church.

The 1,000,000-1 shot has come in.

But a former slots kingpin a major officer of a major church? One of the slots geniuses in the back room now a church decision-maker?

"The obligation for us as a staff," he says "is to conduct ourselves in a manner that somebody, seeing what we're doing, wouldn't say, 'Oh, my gosh, what's going on, how could this guy be doing that?'"

After twenty years in the slots business and five in the employ of the church, Geoff knows better than most that the line between liberality on one hand and legalism on the other can seem very blurry in Vegas. (He might even admit that the city fathers designed it that way.) But as a member of the leadership team in a church with over ten thousand weekly attendees, many of whom work in casinos, he makes good stewardship his overriding standard.

Not long ago the mother who kidnapped him, the one who wanted Geoff when he didn't want her, the one whose perfume and tinted hair and cigarette habit he never liked, died in a nursing home on a hill overlooking Vegas.

It was as if Geoff had come full circle. During her funeral he told a gathering about the kidnappings, about the threadbare apartment in which she lived, about her rough edges and contrarian ways.

There came a time, Geoff said, when he realized that he loved her in the abstract but disliked her in the concrete. And that wasn't good enough. He said God wanted him to genuinely *like* her. So he set about to visit her more frequently, meet her incidental needs and wants, enjoy her company as she smoked. And over time he discovered that he actually began to like her and love her in reality.

It was almost poetic. The decision comes first, Geoff said, and then one's feelings. Just like the workings of faith in a slot-machine man's heart.

CHAPTER TEN

Safe at Home

Scott's Story

Many people come to Las Vegas to play. Some arrive to start a new life.

Scott Reader came to Vegas to die.

He is a small man, five feet six, in his mid-forties. He has salt-and-pepper hair getting grayer on the sides. He is bright, alert, and extremely articulate. Some may consider him glib, but that's because he's a transplanted New Yorker and the words come spilling out in a rush.

He is sitting in a multipurpose room he uses for his volunteer work at Central. Though he has a condominium not far away, the church amounts to his extended home. He spends anywhere from twenty-five to seventy-five hours a week volunteering there.

One of his most disarming qualities is his smile, which hints of shyness.

"My grandmother always told me I had a nice smile," he says. "And it worked with the boys too."

Like almost all Las Vegans, Scott Reader is from somewhere else.

And like tens of thousands of those who come to Vegas, there was trouble in the family back home.

Scott came from a Catholic family of five with a middle-class outlook. They lived on southern Long Island, about forty-five miles from Manhattan. His father was an abusive alcoholic and his mother, caught in the middle, took it out on the kids.

Alcoholism ran in the family—a time-honored Vegas trait. The whole family clung together, holding family gatherings that literally swayed back and forth. People would drink, argue, drink some more, take off in rages and occasionally bang up cars. It was both entertaining and frightful.

Scott was like a possum in those days, just hunkering down and surviving. He liked to draw. And in his private world he sensed how an attractively designed object could catch the eye.

At eighteen he enrolled in interior design at the famous Fashion Institute of New York. In some ways he was more boy than young man, rarely having been away from home. Yet here he was competing with high-energy, creative people from all over the country.

He was terrified, but told no one about it.

And there was something more he kept to himself. He knew by then he was struggling with same-sex desires.

He began to feel them shortly after puberty. He remembers staring for a time at a young man in a mall and wondering why he felt such longing for him. Now, with homosexuals increasingly more comfortable and open about their lifestyles, he was attending a school where probably 50 percent of the men were gay.

"They picked up on the fact that I seemed to fit in with them," Scott recalls. "They kept telling me I was gay. I tried to suppress it, but I couldn't. Finally I went to a gay bar with one of them, went home with someone, and began the process.

"On balance it was an awful experience. See, I now know what same-sex attraction is. I know the reasoning behind it. It's brokenness. All I wanted was someone to take care of me. Unfortunately, in order to get someone to take care of me, I had to give them what they wanted. And they teach you what they want."

Initially Scott had only one-night affairs. *Maybe one of the men I have sex with,* he thought, *will turn out to be Mr. Right.*

"Part of it was feeling accepted and embraced," he recalls. "But I mostly spent the next morning crying on my way home in a cab."

Late in his junior year, though, Scott met a nice guy named Ken, who also was an interior designer. They kind of clicked. And after graduation they moved into an impeccably furnished duplex in midtown Manhattan. There they began what Scott thought would be a monogamous, normal American life—"just two glamorous men in a glamorous city in a glamorous profession."

Just before graduation Scott landed a prestigious job as a designer with Estée Lauder, the cosmetics giant. The job catapulted him into a lifestyle that only the top people of New York enjoy. At twenty-two he was making the highest salary of his college class, had an office at 59th Street and Fifth Avenue, and was designing customized counters and cases costing $100,000 and up. Even better, he was living with a serious boyfriend who fulfilled his every need.

The upscale cosmetics business is a world unto itself. The three giants, Estée Lauder, Lancôme, and Clinique, share the market at the top stores like Bloomingdale's, Macy's, Saks, and Neiman Marcus. Next to jewelry, cosmetics is every store's chief profit center.

Cosmetics selling is all about image—making the counters

and cases shine with their gleaming metals and sparkling glass. Making each look different and better than the next. Customizing everything, making each one curve and glisten, capturing the passing woman's eye. One counter Scott designed cost $1 million.

For all his success, though, Scott was becoming an alcoholic and a drug user.

"I did dope because I didn't become a mess on it," Scott recalls. "I became like a nice vegetable—and it certainly made doing things that were wrong more palatable."

Five years after they became an item, Scott learned that Ken was cheating on the side. When Ken encouraged him to have an affair too, Scott was stunned. "It just seemed gross to me. I didn't want that. I just wanted him. I idolized him."

Soon Ken moved out, and Scott again was needy and alone.

Within a matter of months, though, a woman almost magically appeared in his life. Her name was Cindy. Soon they became intimate both physically and emotionally. They stayed at his expensive new studio apartment all weekend.

"We started to talk about marriage," he remembers. "I wanted what the American dream was. It was the only time in my life I could hold hands publicly. She knew I was gay. And people guessed because there was a nature about me that said 'softer . . . possibly gay.'"

But despite their feelings for each other, it wasn't meant to be. At a George Michael concert one night, Scott found himself staring at the boys. "I said to myself, 'That's it, you're desiring them more than you're desiring her, so what's the use?'"

At the start of the summer he told her he was H.I.V. positive and at the end of the summer he told her he wanted to break up.

Scott was now zero for two in serious relationships—one with a man, one with a woman. But his career continued to blossom. He became one of Estée Lauder's most successful designers, soon making a handsome salary. But he spent far more than he earned, running up huge debts on Caribbean trips, choice clothes, expensive gifts and meals at four-star restaurants.

Within three years Scott became the number two store design director in the nation for Estée Lauder. He still wasn't satisfied. Soon Lancôme, Estée Lauder's arch rival, wooed him away and doubled his pay. A mover and a shaker now, he got a corner office overlooking Fifth Avenue.

Scott quickly went from being an insecure young man to being part of the upper echelon of the homosexual crowd in New York. He went to the "in" places, he wore "in" clothes, and he had the big money.

"It's a very desired life," he says. "It's what you see in all the magazines today. It's what our culture says is the way to live. Very glamorous. Money, clothes, dinners, the best stores, the top-ten lists of places to go and where to be seen.

"I didn't have the best looks or the best body, so you make it up in other ways. You try to be the life of the party. You become very good at sex so you're the one who is desired."

With H.I.V., he didn't care anymore, so he was going to get everything out of life he could. Parties on Fire Island, one-night stands, cocaine, Ecstasy, drinking almost every night of the week—nothing was too much for him.

About a year after he moved to Lancôme, Scott found Peter, another serious lover. Peter was fifteen years older than Scott, an architect and planner for the city government. They lived in Peter's loft—John F. Kennedy Jr. was one of their neighbors—and bought an eleven-room country house in the

Catskills in upstate New York. They entertained there constantly, and the high life was exhilarating in many ways. But at
the end of the night, after the drugs and the sex, Scott was
always devastated emotionally.

One day he found himself in a park in Manhattan watching two guys having a wonderful time doing drugs. He began
thinking about suicide. He thought, *Why am I not like them?
Even if I took more drugs I wouldn't feel any different.*

Without realizing it, Scott was headed for a crash.

A reshuffling of the upper management at Lancôme meant
that Scott's patron, the president, suddenly was out. Scott now
had to report to a new boss—and just a vice president at that.

"I thought I was the most wonderful thing on the face of
the earth. *Screw this,* I said to myself, and quit on the spot."

Everything came spiraling down within the year.

Scott blew through his charge cards like a summer storm.

Peter had to begin supporting him. They put the house
in the Catskills in Peter's name so Scott's creditors couldn't
get at it.

Scott quickly went through a $20,000 advance from Peter
while looking for work, but his confidence was shot and no
one had a spot for him. Finally Peter, pained and broken-
hearted, told him he had to go. For Scott, there was nothing
worse that could happen.

Except, that is, a call from a New York City clinic two
weeks after he had taken one of his periodic H.I.V. tests.

Scott had had the virus that causes AIDS for several years.
The caller simply asked him to come in for a consultation. But
from his contacts in the gay world, Scott knew instantly what
that meant—the H.I.V. had progressed into AIDS.

"It came as a blow to me," he says, "because at that time
AIDS meant death—and death within just a few years. Now

people can live much longer with AIDS because of the medicine that has come out. But back then, the moment they asked me to come in, darkness came over my eyes."

Scott had no idea where to turn. His first beau, Ken, had recently died of AIDS. Ken had been reduced to a skeleton with sickly yellow skin and with damaged nerve endings in his hands and feet that bedeviled him with pain.

Within a few months, though, there was a glimmer of hope. Scott learned that with AIDS he was eligible for Social Security and other payments. But where to live out his last few years?

Scott was estranged from both his brother and father, who had divorced his mother and remarried. Scott's mother, stepfather, and sister, with whom he at least kept in contact, had recently moved to a Vegas retirement community.

The desert it would be.

Scott had never been to Las Vegas.

He was from a city that prided itself on its aesthetic taste. Vegas was a city that had a fifty-four-foot-high casino volcano that erupted every fifteen minutes in a man-made lagoon.

He had been to restaurants in which snow peas were arranged on a plate like a work of art. Most Vegas eateries had no art—just all-you-can-eat buffet lines.

He loved the elegant lines of his display cases and admired fine architecture in public buildings. In the desert there was mainly Vegas architecture—artificial canals worked by ersatz gondoliers, an imitation Eiffel Tower, and a 150-foot-tall Statue of Liberty.

Scott got off the plane at McCarran and was not inspired. "I hated, just hated it," he says.

"It wasn't New York. I didn't like anyplace that wasn't New York. It seemed harsh. It seemed sleazy, with everything based on gambling. *This is a dump*, I thought. *A needle desert.*

"But the only person who would have me was my mother. So my thinking was, I can't show up when I'm a skeleton like Ken was. I might as well show up now so she can have a couple of years with me before I go."

Scott eventually bought a used car and a condo about fifteen minutes from the Strip. The condo was on the edge of Vegas's steadily expanding gay district. With its occasionally seedy bars and storefronts, it was far removed from the lovely shops and boutiques of Chelsea and Greenwich Village in New York. But at least he didn't feel alone.

Scott had been sober since coming down with AIDS and decided that one means of remaining that way was to stay busy. So he helped out with children who had AIDS, pitched in at the city's Gay and Lesbian Center, and joined what's known as "Gay AA."

The burst of activity didn't work.

Eight months after he arrived he resumed life as a binger—this time as a blackout binger, the kind who remembers only bits and pieces of his drinking the night before.

One night Scott started binging somewhere downtown near the north end of the Strip. He remembers finding his way to Las Vegas Boulevard and walking south almost the entire four-mile length of the Strip early in the morning.

He passed the former Treasure Island with the pirate ships in its man-made lagoon. He went by Caesars and the majestic Bellagio, where sometime after daybreak man-made geysers would erupt in the middle of an eleven-acre lagoon.

He kept weaving, past the Aladdin and the MGM Grand and New York–New York, with its roller coaster and Lady

Liberty. He finally approached the southern end of the Strip where the Excalibur stands with its medieval-style castle parapets. Then he passed the pyramid of Luxor, with the searchlight and the giant sphinx guarding the hotel-casino's driveway.

And he remembers seeing none of this.

He was just your occasional stumbling drunk, trying to find a place to flop.

"I ended up in the lobby of one of those cheap hotels a block or two off the Strip," he says. "I didn't have a dime—no wallet, no keys, no coins. And I'm trying to persuade the clerk at the desk to let me use his phone to call my mother.

"I must have been a little incoherent. I can remember the guy at the desk looking at me like, *Oh, here's another one.*

"He must have let me call, though, because I remember talking to my mother. She and my stepfather came down, put me in their car and put me to bed at their place. Then at one point she came in and said, 'I'm not going to put up with the same thing from you I put up with from your father.'"

For awhile, though, nothing changed.

One afternoon he left a Gay AA meeting, went straight to a bar and ordered a drink. He was thinking, *I've just been to AA, how can I do this?* Then he ordered another.

The bar was in a ramshackle area of Vegas not far from the Stratosphere and Frontier Street.

"I ended up meeting this street person there," Scott recalls. "He was an IV user, the kind of guy who works the bars, preying on drunks like I used to be. We started talking, had some drinks and I took him home to my condo.

"I'm sitting there shooting his stuff, something that was probably speed, into my arms. And I've crossed now every line you can cross. I know I have AIDS. I know I'm not supposed to be shooting up. And we're sharing his needle now. I'd been trained in the AIDS world that you never share a needle."

The drifter stayed for a couple of days, taking Scott's cash and hocking his TV, stereo, jewelry, and anything else of value to buy more drugs. Scott eventually called a Gay AA friend to come over and make the guy leave.

Scott had truly hit rock-bottom now. But in God's economy, he was on the way up.

To this day he can't explain it, but he had been drinking and then shooting up for two days without getting messed up. The booze and the drugs simply weren't allowing him to get high enough anymore.

Within a week of his encounter with the drifter, Scott was back in another Gay AA meeting. A heterosexual had been invited to speak. Dennis was a tall, articulate man who taught that at the root of alcoholism was a problem of both the body and the mind, a consuming obsession that alcoholics can rarely, if ever, escape on their own.

Scott immediately understood. He had lived it.

Then Dennis said the problem of the body and the problem of the mind can only be solved *spiritually*. One must turn to a higher power—a power outside oneself. Scott knew deep down that this "higher power" was just a more publicly acceptable term for God, even if AA didn't call it that.

Scott asked Dennis to become his AA sponsor and lead him through the famous twelve-step program.

With the link to AA, heaven had opened just a crack.

Scott had once attended AA meetings at Central. Looking to connect somewhere spiritually, he eventually decided to go there.

It was culture shock.

"When I walked in and saw the big TV screens on the sides of the stage, I thought, *Holy crap, Jim and Tammy Faye Bakker are coming out*," Scott says. "*What is this? Where's the cross? Where's the stained glass? Movie theater seats?* Totally the antithesis of what I knew of church.

"And then they make you stand up and sing. But soon I began to think it was kind of cool because the words to the songs are up there on the screen—you don't have to be embarrassed not knowing them.

"And I had another reaction I'll never forget," Scott says. "The pastor came out and talked about people who were hurting. And I felt as though he was reaching right across the big room and talking to me. He began to well up. And I'm saying to myself, *The guy's going to cry on stage. Please don't cry.* And all the while I'm about to cry myself."

It was his first link to a place in Vegas where he could belong. Obviously, the place was filled with people who were hurting—otherwise, why the pastor's message? Maybe he wasn't the only one whose life was a wreck.

Scott saw in the bulletin that the church had a course on the essentials of the Christian faith that was a prerequisite for membership. He signed up for it and whipped through it in a month and a half. Then he moved into another course that led to adult baptism and becoming a member.

He noticed that baptism seemed extremely unusual at first. But as others were baptized it struck Scott as oddly appealing.

"Most of the people in the class were couples," Scott recalls. "And I'm a little uncomfortable because I'm gay. I'm already saying to myself, *I'll bet you gay isn't very popular here.*

"No one said anything because it's not the kind of church

that criticizes people for their past. And no one's giving me any long looks like I didn't belong there. But at this time I'm not planning on leaving the gay life. I wasn't having much sex—hardly any, in fact—but I didn't think there was any problem with remaining in the gay life.

"I was going to have God *and* homosexuality."

Scott now had a Bible. One night, doing some homework before his class the next day, he saw that it had an appendix for words and subjects. *Oh,* he thought, *I wonder what it says about homosexuality?*

"I went to the Old Testament first," Scott says. "And when it talked about death in regard to homosexuality, I figured, *Well, this can be true; homosexuals do die if they get AIDS.* Then I saw a verse that says homosexuals should be *put* to death. Now that was something else. That was hard for me."

Scott went in to see one of the pastors the next morning and told him about his homosexuality. Fortunately for Scott, the pastor advised that they focus on the New Testament first.

There Scott learned that the message Jesus came to preach was not condemning, but liberating. Scott read with his own eyes that when a person puts his trust in Christ there is total and complete freedom from the penalty for one's sins.

Under the law, which is spelled out in the Old Testament, there definitely was condemnation—and it *was* scary. But Scott began to understand that Jesus took upon Himself the penalty of the old law so that people like him could be free at last.

And equally important to Scott, the pastor explained that what Scott *did* was one thing. Who he *was,* was another.

"For me, as for most gay people," Scott says, "being gay was my own identity. It was everything to me—my work, my clothes, my social life. I never had it explained to me that maybe I had sexual practices that were homosexual, but that what I was doing didn't have to be who I was."

Scott and the pastor started talking about Scott's getting baptized, but something wouldn't let him. His heart wasn't settled. And what would have been a big step forward suddenly seemed like two steps back.

Scott called Dennis and some of their AA friends. He told them about his conference at Central.

Scott remembers the scene exactly:

"Now Dennis, a heterosexual, says to me, 'Scott, there are two types of homosexuals. There are those who have become homosexuals because of circumstance. And there are those who are born that way.'

"He then says, 'Scott, I believe you were born that way.'

"So I've got a pastor on one hand. And I have only AA friends on the other—all of them very worldly, probably more worldly than most worldly people, completely liberal. And most of them are now telling me, 'It's this church you're going to. They're wrong! You are who you are. You should love yourself the way you are.'"

Scott had had it with Dennis, who taught him so much about sobriety but was so directive. And with Central, because now he couldn't picture it. If he was gay and wanted to marry some man and maybe even adopt children, how could they all walk in next to all the heterosexual married couples there?

So soon he attended a congregation for gays in Vegas. But it wasn't what he expected.

"Their teaching that you could have Christ and the Bible and homosexuality all at the same time had exactly the opposite effect on me," Scott recalls. "Here I'm trying to be convinced that they had the right way to go, yet I'm being *unconvinced.* Every bit of their proof turned me further away.

"I began to sit there and make a distinction. I thought, *Well, at Central you walk in and it's happy.* You at least see bright faces and people are taking care of you. At the gay church everyone looked depressed. I began thinking that people whacked out on drugs in discos at four o'clock in the morning actually looked more cheerful than people at the gay church.

"The last straw was when the main speaker would start talking. It was so boring and meaningless it took every ounce of my strength not to pass out. Week after week I'd fight to keep from nodding off. Finally I decided, *Well, forget this, I'm not going back.*"

Scott decided to return to Central. Only this time he took the advice of his AA friends to sit in the back up near the rafters and not get involved. He should enjoy but not participate. They told him that no one assumes you come to get involved in a church. You just sit there and take what you want.

His first time back, Scott took the most remote seat in the church he could find. But a strange thing happened. The pastor who had been able to reach across the room and connect with him before did the same thing again—only this time on a deeper level.

He was preaching a series of messages on broken relationships. The talks may have been designed for heterosexuals, but somehow it didn't matter. Scott was disarmed, brushing tears from his eyes throughout.

Two weeks later Scott had moved down to his old seat in row 7, center section, twenty-five feet from the stage. He found himself feeling at home.

He was surrounded by couples, singles, twentysomethings, middle-agers, and even the occasional senior. What they obviously had in common was this: No matter how short of the mark they had fallen yesterday or last year or a decade ago, no matter how heavy or light their baggage, they each knew they were part of God's family if they had put their trust in Christ.

For the first time he found himself relating to others at Central. There seemed to be a commonality about the place, even though there were thousands attending. Was it because almost everybody admitted they were broken? That they all needed help? He couldn't put his finger on it, but there was an intangible they seemed to share—an energy and authenticity about the place.

By now Scott was determined to stay. He knew it was a church he could call home. There seemed to be few, if any, pretensions. Lord knows, he had been living with enough of those.

Besides, he wanted to be part of a community in his life. His forty or so years had been a sea of impermanent relationships. What he needed at this stage was reality and connectedness. A place where he could help others, use his talents, and be loved in return.

After the service he met the pastor he had spoken with weeks before. He hadn't thought about changing his sexual orientation. But for some reason he found himself saying he needed to see the pastor again. They made an appointment for a couple of weeks away.

Little did Scott know that God would soon be knocking at his door.

Back at his condo, he began reading a short book by a nineteenth-century Scottish evangelical writer and speaker named Henry Drummond that had been popular decades ago in AA circles. It was entitled *The Greatest Thing in the World* and talked about the sheer power of Jesus.

Scott had always assumed God was powerful, in the remote

kind of way that one assumes the cosmos is vast, but he had never reckoned with the personal power of God through Christ. While he was reading, the thought suddenly occurred to him that he had no more desire to drink. He was overwhelmed by the realization—the desire had completely vanished. And he knew as well as he knew his own name that it was God who had removed it.

He began to think about other aspects of his life.

The desire to do drugs? *Suddenly gone.*

The desire to swear at his parents when they angered him? "There were points in my life when I said some awful stuff to them, and I wasn't ashamed about it either," he says—that was gone as well. And now replaced with a surprising desire to treat them as worthy of his respect.

The desire to lie, cheat, and steal? The compulsion to smoke, abuse alcohol, and hand over his body to all kinds of drugs? Yes, those desires were gone too.

The reality that God had removed these cravings for more than a year now washed over him. He became overwhelmed by the notion of God's sheer power. And in the logical progression of his mind, he began to think the impossible. If God had taken away these desires, could He go a step further and remove Scott's desire for other men?

"I've done way more than you even know because of the darkness of the homosexual life and the lines one crosses," Scott says.

"But that was my thought. And you know what happened? I was quickly overwhelmed with the sense that based upon my life, yes, He could. Look what He had done for me already. So of course He was powerful enough."

Scott Reader is a logician if nothing else.

Then obviously there was a follow-up question.

"The next thought that came into my head—and I'll thank God forever for leading me to it—was *do I want Him to?* To me it was an amazing question. Because just because I realized God *could* do it, did I really want to give this up?"

Again, the answer came within seconds.

Yes, of course I want God to remove these desires! Scott thought.

Scott remembers at that moment looking at his life as a homosexual. He knew that his AIDS was the direct result of promiscuous behavior. So there he was, sitting alone in a Vegas condo with hardly any gay friends, with no male lover, this so-called life that he had hoped for and dreamed of having never panned out.

"I knew it was God," he says. "And so I thought, *Well of course I want to give this up.* It was a no-brainer.

"I had always throughout AA prayed morning and evening on my knees at my bedside—I still do. So I knew immediately to go from the sofa into the bedroom and get on my knees and pray to God to please remove my desire to be attracted to men. And there the process began."

It so happened that the following morning Scott had his previously scheduled meeting at church. Scott decided he needed to be baptized to come to terms with his own sexuality. He needed to mark the break from his past.

Scott chose to be baptized and invite many of his AA friends and family members to come for what he knew would be his greatest celebration. All but his mother declined to attend.

Scott Reader came to Las Vegas to die and found fullness of life instead.

He has overcome so much in his addiction to drugs and alcohol. He has helped dozens of people face their same-sex attractions and find healing. And he has Christ as an advocate and a very present help in time of trouble.

But his life is not perfect by a long shot. And these truths do not mean he is immune to temptation. And of course, Scott still has AIDS. And someday he may die of it. He knows what that's like, having watched his former lover Ken. But he's not afraid.

"What's the worst thing that could happen? You die? Actually, with God, that's a good thing.

"Because there's hope no matter what.

"There's a creator. And that creator loves us.

"He has designed a reason for our existence.

"There are still rough spots from time to time, but I have meaning, despite what somebody else may say I am.

"And there's a reason to be obedient because of God's great love."

A Place to Belong

What do you do in Vegas?" the waitress in Virginia asked as she looked at my license.

"I'm a pastor at a church," I said.

"No you aren't," she fired back.

"Yes, I am," I replied.

"No, you aren't," she said matter-of-factly. "There are *no* churches in Las Vegas."

Her certainty was absolute. After five minutes I gave up trying to convince her that churches can and do exist in unlikely places, and minister to unlikely people. Her perception of the church just could not make room for Vegas.

When you hear the word "church," what comes to your mind? Do you think of stained glass and steeples or a remodeled warehouse? Do you hear organ music or rock and roll? Do you see Maude Flanders from *The Simpsons* or the church lady from *Saturday Night Live*? There are a lot of different pictures that come to mind for each of us.

As a teenager I didn't understand why people attended church. My parents were true believers. They went to church every weekend and dragged me along. As they attended the main service, I convinced them that I went to youth group. In reality I'd slip out the back door and walk the alleys around the church, smoking cigarettes and waiting for the service to end.

I felt like an outsider as I watched people pull into the church parking lot and walk into the building. Some looked happy and were excited to be there, some looked frustrated, and some looked tired and bored. *What's the point?* I wondered. In a world filled with injustice, corruption, and death, how could God exist anyway? If He was so great, then why was the world so messed up? And what honest difference could God make in my life?

I'd hear Christians talk about heaven and hell, but from my vantage point at the time, hell didn't seem so bad. If hell was real, and the Christians were right, then all my friends would end up there anyway. And if heaven was populated by some of the people who claimed they knew the way, I wasn't sure I wanted to be with them.

So I skipped church each week. Yet something pulled on my heart. I sensed that I was not right with the world, that there was more to life. When I finally turned to God and asked for help, I walked across the parking lot and into that church. I certainly didn't have all the answers, but for the first time I was genuinely open to exploring my questions.

God, through the people of the church, saved my life. I never recovered from how those people helped me and prayed for me when I was broken and confused. That's what the church should do, what it should be. And that's why I've dedicated my life to helping others who are like me. Walking across that parking lot that day is a decision I have never regretted. As I think of my journey—or that of Geoff Sage or Scott Reader or thousands of others—I realize we all found healing and help through the *community of people called the church*. We found love, acceptance, and grace. And we experienced God's dream for the church—and the world—in a very personal way.

From the beginning, God's dream involved community and friendship. The Bible says, "Long before he laid down earth's foundations, he had us in mind, had settled on us as the focus of his love, to be made whole and holy by his love" (Ephesians 1:4, *The Message*). We were created in love, with love, and by love. (This may seem too good to be true, but I've come to believe it precisely because it *is* so good it *must* be true. God spoke creation into being so that we could join His fellowship.)

When God created people, He said, "Let *us* make man in *our* image" (Genesis 1:26). Who exactly is "us"? No one was created yet, but God was in community with Himself. The Bible shows God in a community of love, peace, and fulfillment even before the first human comes into being.

I admit this is challenging to grasp. (Of course, if it were not challenging to grasp, it would be hard to believe this is God we are talking about.) A word in Genesis might help us begin to understand. The Hebrew term for God in Genesis 1 is *Elohim*, which is plural in form, but singular in meaning. We read in Genesis 1:1 of God, the Creator of the heavens and the earth. In verse 2, the Spirit of God hovers over the waters like a protector, and in verse 3, the Word of God speaks order to creation. Later John would write, "In the beginning was the Word, and the Word…became flesh and made his dwelling among us" in Jesus (John 1:1, 14). God creates, the Spirit protects, and the Word implements His will. Even in the first three verses of the Bible we see a trinity of God the Father, the Spirit, and the Son. They are in community. And Adam is created to join God's community.

Seven times in chapter 1 of Genesis God looks out at His creation and notes that it is good. Yet when He creates Adam, He says it isn't good he is alone. Even though Adam was in a relationship with God, this was not enough. For a time after I became a Christian, I thought that all I needed was God. Yet according to God Himself, I was wrong. I needed more than God. I needed others, just as Adam did. So God creates the woman as a "helpmate" for Adam. Behind the Hebrew noun "helper" is the verb "to save." Eve is created as a savior, Adam's rescuer from solitude.

The Bible is the story of God's dream for community coming to fruition. He starts with Adam and Eve and later calls together a people, Israel, and unites them as His own to enjoy each other and His fellowship. They are to shine the light of His love and goodness to the world. Then Jesus comes and begins a new community through His death, resurrection, and ascension to heaven. The community of the church is born, a fellowship of diverse people with a common Lord and goal.

I believe with all my heart that the church is the world's hope. Government can't change the heart. Education, as important as it is, can't change the heart. Healthcare and Social Security reform won't change the heart. Only God can do that. And He uses people—*the church*—to reach out and impact others. Many people are cynical and skeptical about the church. And who can deny all the scandals and hypocrisy that occur in the name of God? It is truly awful. Yet, for every scandal there are thousands and thousands of churches making a real difference and doing their best to help others.

Critiques and cynicism without solutions don't help anyone. I get weary of idealistic visions of a church community so perfect and pompous that the person telling me of this church wouldn't even fit in—they'd have too many issues!

My mother always said, "The church would be a perfect place if there weren't any people in it." People—people like you and me—are the problem. Some think the answer is in the size of a church—from a house church to a midsize church to a megachurch. Others think the secret is in the style of ministry, from traditional to emerging. No matter how you view it, every church community will be messy because it is filled with imperfect people, imperfectly following Jesus. These people may be the problem—but they can also be the solution. Yes, life is messy. Church is messy. Faith is messy. But let's get over it, and get on with helping people experience God's grace.

Many churches, in an attempt to deal with this messiness head-on, have come to value a sense of *belonging* as primary. Some churches taught (and still teach) that first you *believe*, then you *behave*, and finally you *belong*. For these churches, belief in Christ is the first step in being part of a church, but you do not really belong until you behave.[14] But many churches are more or less reversing this order out of a love for people far from God. Their philosophy is first you belong, then you believe, and finally you behave.

Sometimes a person belongs for months or even years before they believe. On any given weekend at Central, there are hundreds of people who would not define themselves as Christians if you asked them. I have friends who attend every weekend who are Jewish and do not yet place faith in Jesus. Or they are agnostic, but like the music. They may be a mix of many religions, but they sense the place is real. They are searching. They belong first, and my prayer is one day they will believe. We are honest and straightforward about sin and salvation through the person of Jesus. We do not water down the Bible or the teachings of Christ, but we do accommodate in every other way possible. We love people no matter where they are. Out of that love, life-change will eventually occur.

Paul describes the all-encompassing, radical counterculture of the church of God, the called out ones who place their faith in Jesus, like this: "There is neither Jew nor Greek, slave nor free, male nor female," he says, "for you are all one in Christ Jesus" (Galatians 3:28). In the church, there is no place for prejudice between rich and poor, black and white, educated and uneducated, clean and dirty, male and female, even Dallas Cowboys fans and Pittsburgh Steelers fans—we are all united in Christ!

Thomas Cahill, in his book *The Desire for the Everlasting Hills*, suggests that Paul in Galatians 3:28 is the first writer in the history of world literature to argue for the true equality of all human beings.[15] Wow! The church is a place where the social stigmas that divide us in our culture fade. It is a place where hope and healing are experienced, where grace flows freely and new life is found. And there are no requirements to get in the door. This is God's idea, the new community called out to serve Christ and impact the world.

What should we do to have impact on the people around us? We need to look no further than Christ, our perfect Teacher. The greatest commandments according to Jesus are to love God and "love your neighbor as yourself" (Mark 12:31). He did not say to love your neighbor if you are in the mood, or if she likes the same hobbies, or if he believes the same things you do. He just says love them. Period. Irrespective of their background and history, Jesus loves them and so should we.

I know of a woman who relocated to Vegas with her husband, only to find her happiness slipping away six months after they arrived. She felt that her marriage, along with the rest of her life, was falling apart. It all came to a head one afternoon, and she sat in a grocery store parking lot with her head down and wept. Suddenly a stranger knocked on her window and said, "Ma'am, I don't know what is wrong, but I can tell that you are hurting. You should go to my church. They will help you there."

The woman got directions and drove from the grocery store to Central. What changed her life was not the building, but the people inside. They led her that day into a relationship with Jesus. She was back that weekend with her husband, and as the months went on they credited the people of the church for significantly turning their life and relationship around. This is the church at its best, helping and loving people one at a time.

Jesus' number one emotional response mentioned in the Gospels is compassion. This is astounding when we consider that Jesus was sinless, but constantly surrounded by sin and sinful people. Sin violently opposed His character. Everywhere He turned He saw the effects of injustice and hate. It would have been easy for Jesus to blast people for their mistakes. He had more right than anyone to take a political and moral stand, to picket on the street, form protests, and publicly attack individuals.

Yet we read that when Jesus "saw the crowds, he had compassion on them, because they were harassed and helpless, like sheep without a shepherd" (Matthew 9:36). Jesus saw people as sheep that have been bruised, beaten, and thrown to and fro. Rather than being filled with disdain, He was filled with love.

As the most spiritually mature person to ever live, Jesus stands as *the* model for what a spiritual life looks like. He remained approachable to outsiders and the hurting. His life reveals that the more spiritually mature I am, the more approachable I am to people who feel far from God. As spiritual maturity increases, approachability increases.[16] It is a sad indictment that many outside the faith don't feel like they can approach Christians. In Jesus' day, some of the least approachable people were the religious leaders. They reeked of self-righteousness and judgment. Yet Jesus' life should give us pause: *Am I truly approachable to all kinds of people? Do I have the compassion of Jesus for those who are hurting or disillusioned? Is that compassion evident to others?*

Studies show that the primary things many younger Americans think when they hear the word "Christian" are 1) anti-homosexual and 2) anti-abortion.[17] Something is very wrong. Their entire perception of Christianity centers on what it is against. How far we have strayed from Jesus! I pray in twenty years the same survey will reveal the number one thing people think about Christians is that they love others. Certainly love and compassion characterize Jesus and should characterize us.

Scott Reader and Geoff Sage experienced life change as they belonged to a faith community that shared Jesus' love with them. It was a process for each of them just as it was for me. Part of grace is giving people the space to journey things out. For fallen people like you and me, change comes slowly, and we need to be helped along by loving hands.

A few years ago I visited a gay man dying of AIDS in a hospice. Our church cared for him in his last days, and his homosexual friends witnessed this. When others turned away, we turned toward him in compassion, and we stood beside him. After his death, one of his dearest friends asked, "Would you mind if we attend your church?"

He was so moved by our compassion and care that he wanted to be part of our community. I, along with others, enthusiastically encouraged him to attend and feel welcome. He also understood that we viewed homosexual behavior as sin, but he saw in our actions that we really did care about people. He did attend, and later he became a follower of Jesus.

That's the power of God's grace working in our lives. That is the power of belonging that led us to create a culture at Central where it is okay to not be okay.[18] You don't have to pretend you have it together if you don't. Just come as you are, with your past, pain, challenges, and junk. God promises to meet you where you are, but He won't leave you there. He'll begin a work of transformation in your life.

Today is Sunday, and as I walked into church around 6:30 a.m., I saw the homeless lined up outside the resource area. We have groups that serve the homeless in our community and others who serve them on our campus, where they receive clean clothes and basic necessities. Sometimes I stand back and watch as volunteers joke with them, giving them dignity and showing them respect. They laugh, hug, and try to encourage. Do the volunteers realize that every act of kindness toward these downtrodden people is an act of kindness toward Jesus?

Jesus once told a story of people rewarded by God after this life. They were praised because, as He put it, "I was hungry and you gave me something to eat, I was thirsty and you gave me something to drink, I was a stranger and you invited me in, I needed clothes and you clothed me, I was sick and you looked after me, I was in prison and you came to visit me." The people were confused and asked Jesus when they saw him hungry or in need. He replied, "I tell you the truth, whatever you did for one of the least of these brothers of mine, you did for me" (Matthew 25:35–36, 40). In these words is the fullness of God's dream for us—when we are in communion with one another, we are in communion with Him.

For years I've heard teaching about how believers experience Jesus' presence in the bread and cup of communion. I've been taught that it is a mysterious and sacred experience. I've sought Jesus' presence in communion and counseled others to do the same. Yet only once, at the Last Supper, did Jesus tell us of His presence in the bread and cup. More often He spoke of His presence in the poor and downcast.[19] But for all the messages I've heard about communion, I've rarely heard about Jesus' presence in helping others. Both communion and meeting needs are avenues that allow me to experience His presence. In helping others, my focus is shifted from my own problems and pain to those in need around me, and it changes both me and them for the better. Jesus' presence in the smallest acts can make a huge impact.

I know one woman who would attest to this truth. Gabriella struggled with all kinds of medical complications without insurance, and it drained her resources. Through a series of circumstances, she bottomed out, living in her car with her two young children. Eventually she scraped together enough money to rent a room by the week at a cheap motel. School began, and all she could give her children in the way of supplies were two pencils. Sending them off to school, she made a decision to prostitute herself that night to get money to take care of her kids.

She had asked God to help her, but had resigned herself

to the fact that He would not. Feeling completely deserted by God, she made arrangements for the kids to be watched that evening and waited for them to get out of school. She would do what she had to do.

When they came home, she was shocked to see they each had brand-new backpacks filled with school supplies. She asked where they came from, and the kids indicated they received them from their school. Her daughter reached into the backpack and pulled out a letter explaining that the backpacks and supplies were a gift from our church. Gabriella clutched that letter to her heart, and for the first time in years, she believed that God had not abandoned them.

She then decided not to work the streets that night. Maybe there was a God after all, and maybe, just maybe, He cared. Gabriella found a phone and called the church to say thank you. When a staff member heard her story, she was touched. She worked with her and helped her find a job and get into an apartment over the next several weeks. Gabriella found, in Central, a place to belong, and eventually, she placed her faith in Christ. I can still see her smile the night she was baptized.

There are plenty of things I don't fully understand in the Bible, but it is clear to me how God feels about the community of people called the church. He loves the church and calls the church to share His love through small and large acts of kindness. Everyone plays a part. If you want to find God in Vegas or anywhere else, you don't have to look for a burning bush or parting water. He is present in every suffering person you meet. You need only to reach out to them—and you will also be reaching out to Him.

In soup kitchens across the world, as people reach out, Jesus is present. In hospitals, as health workers go the extra mile to provide care, He is present. In legal offices as lawyers do pro bono legal work for the needy, He is present. As Scott Reader helps others sorting through same-sex attraction, He is present. As Geoff Sage leads and prays and plans, He is present. In the simple things….a backpack…a hug…a card…a phone call, Jesus is present. He is impacting the world through this ragtag group of followers known as the church. I'm just grateful to be part of it.

PART FOUR: AMAZING GRACE

CHAPTER TWELVE

Officer Down

Henry's Story

4:30 a.m., Wednesday, February 1, 2006

Henry Prendes had come home to his wife with a migraine the evening before. His stomach had been queasy and he had gone straight to bed. Dawn, his wife of two years, had gently massaged his temples and rubbed his eyes to ease the throbbing.

Now, two hours before daybreak, he was up and restless as usual.

A bull of a man—five feet ten and 215 pounds, with a neck the size of a tree trunk—he pulled on sweatpants and a T-shirt, which he invariably wore to Metro's Southwest Command headquarters on Spring Mountain Road near Chinatown. There he would change into his police sergeant's uniform before conducting the six forty-five squad briefing.

He walked into the family room of the big house in northwest Vegas. He had moved in when he married Dawn, two years after his divorce became final. And his teenaged girls, Brooke and Kylee, now spent much of their time there as well. It was the largest home they had ever had, the fruit of several years Dawn spent as senior vice president and chief financial officer of the Golden Nugget downtown.

Henry, thirty-seven, and Dawn, forty-one, were avid golfers—they were building an even larger ten-thousand-square-foot home overlooking a Jack Nicklaus course in Summerlin. And the following day Henry and two of his golf buddies were leaving for their annual outing at the Phoenix Open in Arizona.

Henry pulled out his cell and called his mother in Miami. His mom, a native of Spain, and his dad, an anti-Castro Cuban, had come first to Florida and then to Vegas decades before. They put down roots in the blue-collar neighborhood near Charleston and Lamb, and Henry had become class president and a star linebacker at Las Vegas High. But his father died suddenly when Henry was twenty, and his mother returned to Miami. His biggest regret was he called her so seldom. But they connected now, and it brightened his mood. He promised he would call her back in the afternoon.

Brooke was still in her bed when Henry kissed Dawn good-bye. Kylee was at her mother's home—the girls occasionally took turns staying at either parent's place.

This was going to be a special day, Henry thought. His mood was so buoyant that he left his Jeep in the driveway and took Dawn's BMW to the stationhouse for the first time. Nothing like driving in comfort.

7:10 a.m.

It had been a quiet night in the Southwest district, so Henry and another sergeant had combined their squads and were wrapping up the morning briefing.

Henry had started in patrol just two weeks before, after spending five years in sexual assault. It had been hard work dealing with rapes, abuse, and crimes against children. And his view of both human nature and Vegas on the underside was not pretty. Now, in patrol, he was more of an administrator, floating in and out of the stationhouse while on the phone with eight other officers who drove the streets.

One of the sixteen patrol officers in the room was thirty-year-old Jason Hansen. He and Henry had grown up not far from each other when Vegas was so much smaller. Jason was just as underprivileged as Henry, having grown up in a trailer park.

He is a stocky, baby-faced guy whose ruddy complexion makes him look as if he has just spent a day in the Vegas sun after three years inside his house. After making it through high school, he knocked around for several years, working in construction and other low-paying jobs.

Jason had always admired Henry from afar, even rooming for awhile with one of Henry's best friends. Some years before, Henry had helped him land a health club job. But eventually Jason got married and, facing new responsibilities, decided to become a cop.

He worked in Northeast Command, one of the most dangerous precincts in Vegas. Ensconced in a new house and with his first son having just arrived, he had recently transferred to the much safer Southwest headquarters. Just the previous Thursday he had reintroduced himself to Henry. In typical Prendes fashion, Henry had urged him to come to his Bible study group that evening. Jason had taken a rain check for the following week's meeting.

That meeting was now one day away. "Sarge," Jason said as they left the briefing, "you still doing that Bible study tomorrow?"

Henry was always recruiting, never missing an opportunity. "Yeah, man," he said. "And you need to be there."

7:35 a.m.

"Hey, you up for breakfast?" Henry was on his cell to Danny Garcia, one of his boyhood pals from the neighborhood.

Danny went way back with Henry. He and Henry, along with Pedro Ratchet and Bobby Ozuna, had been like brothers—pals as long as they could remember, attending the same schools, seeing the same circle of girls, playing sports, lifting weights, and even wearing each others' clothes when money was tight.

Back in the mideighties, when they were teenagers doing typically teenaged things, Bobby's uncle, Art Muñoz, decided they needed something. He packed them into a van and drove to Camp Woodleaf in California, not far from Tahoe. Woodleaf was run by a national Christian ministry. And there in the high country Uncle Art's dream came true—all four heard the gospel message and invited Christ into their hearts.

A week after they got back to Vegas, Art took the guys onto the Strip to pass out religious pamphlets. Henry became a team unto himself, chasing down pedestrians, sticking pamphlets in their hands, and telling them that God was still God in Sin City. It was a window into his personality. He was proactive to the core, assertive, persistent, willing to confront others for their ultimate good.

Two of Danny's favorite stories were about Henry doing what Henry did best.

One day while on duty, Henry discovered a young couple and their child living in their car in a fenced-off lot. From the conditions inside the car, they obviously had been there for a month or more. Henry could have arrested them for vagrancy—and, in the process, broken up the family. He gave them directions to an aid center instead. Then he removed a

$20 bill from his wallet and said, "Here, take this, you need it."

Then there was the time when Uncle Art and Henry worked together to arrest a prostitute—and to tell her about the gospel. Henry was on the vice unit then, working at the Rio. He got the prostitute to approach Art while he was sitting at the bar. Then, as the three of them rode up in the elevator, Henry asked whether she took the Gold Card. When she said yes, Henry showed her his badge and made the arrest. But then, Art gently told her about God's plan of salvation.

Now, sitting at a table in Egg Works, Danny, Henry, and Lt. Jeff Carlson, Henry's supervisor, ordered omelets. Henry got the usual—egg whites for his health, coffee for his adrenaline, potatoes and diced chicken mixed in because you can't give up everything.

The conversation got around to Metro's former sheriff, who had landed the sweet job as chief of security at Steve Wynn's Vegas resorts. The Super Bowl was just five days off, so they debated the merits of the Steelers and the Seahawks. Henry was a Cowboys fanatic. Had Dallas been in it, he might have been headed to the game that very hour.

10:30 a.m.

Amir Crump sat on the end of his bed at his girlfriend's house on Feather Duster Court near I-215 in far western Vegas. His friend, Hakeem Robinson, was in the room with him. The girlfriend, Pilar Ramirez, who worked as a "professional model" (which is a Vegas euphemism for someone who poses for sex-magazine photos) and exotic dancer, was downstairs with her mother, whispering as she usually did when Crump was edgy.

Crump, or "Trajik," as he was known in local rap circles, had been trying to write some more lyrics for his latest song, but the words weren't coming to him. He had not been able to concentrate since the previous afternoon when he and Robinson had returned with a new supply of Ecstasy, a powerful hallucinogenic.

Now, on the bed with the door closed, he swallowed a pill, and it wasn't long before the familiar rush began. It normally was a wonderful high, but this time he was edgy and irritable because he had previously taken nearly twice the level of meth sufficient to kill an adult. In the closet was a fully loaded knockoff AK-47 assault rifle and several hundred rounds of extra ammunition.

Pilar had better stop dissing him, he thought. If she and her mother played with his head any longer, they'd better look out, man, because this was Trajik they were messing with.

10:35 a.m.

Henry's cell buzzed while he was at his new home site, checking on the contractors and handling calls from the station. It was his friend Ted Buchman. Ted was wondering if Henry had brought to work a DVD he'd promised during a second Bible study at his house on Sunday night.

Ted was an all-Nevada linebacker at Chaparral High a few years after Henry was all-Clark County at Las Vegas. Playing golf with him the previous week, Ted had discussed some financial trouble and family problems he'd been having with his sister and others. He had been moved when Henry stopped on the spot, put his arm around him, and prayed.

They decided to meet in twenty minutes at Bass Pro Shop, off I-15. The store has a deep lot, and by the time Ted arrived,

Henry was parked in the back, as if he were watching the store. He seemed reflective, which for him was somewhat out of character.

Ted would have hopped into the front seat, except he didn't want to move Henry's Bible, which lay open there. Henry carried it in his car and, when appropriate, referred to it on his rounds. He had been reading it when Ted pulled up.

Soon Henry began joking about what would happen if he "scoped" Ted—looked up his name on the traffic and police computer in his car. He plugged in Ted's Social Security number. Instantly, up popped a '98 ticket for an illegal turn and a '00 ticket for speeding. "Geez," Henry said in mock alarm, looking at him as if he were a convicted felon.

Then Henry changed the subject with some words that still echo in Ted's mind: "Hey, bro, you need to make peace with your sister and lead her to the Lord. And you really need to become a regular at the small group."

Ted and Henry shook hands through the car window and departed. Later in the day, the handshake reminded Ted of the final time he had held his grandmother's hand a dozen years before.

11:30 a.m.

Dawn's cell buzzed on the counter in her kitchen just as a couple of visitors were about to take home two of the three puppies her Rottweiler had delivered. It was Henry. And it was an odd moment because neither of them totally wanted to give the puppies away.

Henry sensed it and began playing on her emotions. "Oh," he teased, "you're not going to be able to get rid of them. You love them too much."

"Yes I am," she shot back. "*You're* not going to be able to!" After all, it was he who played with the puppies every night, and it was she who cleaned up after them.

Dawn and Henry were approaching their two-year anniversary. He furnished spiritual direction for her and became, however briefly, the soul mate of her life. She provided balance for him, not to mention the love he needed after the worst passage of his life.

In 1999 Henry's marriage to his junior high sweetheart and the mother of his girls had hit the wall. He viewed marriage as a sacred covenant, but all attempts at reconciliation failed. Still believing but no doubt wondering where God was, he turned to women and the Vegas night scene.

By 2001, when his divorce became final, Henry had gone from being a straight-and-narrow to a thirtysomething party guy. He professed faith in Christ but was living on the other side of the mountain. He ditched Bible studies and regular church attendance. His life outside work became a round of gambling at the poker table and the $1 slots, drinking and womanizing—especially the womanizing. He sometimes separately dated two women a night and hit the town with dozens of them that year.

Finally, his mentors in the faith—Uncle Art and two friends from Central, whose small group he had attended—did the Christian equivalent of gang-tackling him. His lifestyle, they said, was inconsistent with the gospel.

Surprisingly, he not only listened but obeyed. It was as if he had been yearning to be corrected. Abruptly changing his ways, he returned to church and got back to his daily fix—the Scriptures.

Early in 2003 a mutual policewoman friend introduced Dawn and Henry to each other. It was a little awkward; they weren't teenagers.

"What are you doing setting me up with a guy who's got kids?" Dawn joked to her friend. But Henry was an open, transparent man—you felt as if you knew him the moment you met. They took their first trip together in June, to her hometown of Chicago. He asked her to marry him on his thirty-fifth birthday, December 31, and they were married nine weeks later.

Now, on the phone, they found themselves discussing arrangements to buy a seventeen-acre campsite in Montana that would become a new Woodleaf. Think big was their motto. Kids like Henry would find new lives there. It was a plan that had been consuming them for months.

Soon the new owners of the puppies were getting fidgety in the kitchen.

"I'd better go," Dawn said. "Talk to you later."

12:45 p.m.

Back on Feather Duster Court, Pilar had just had it out with Crump. She had accused him of being unfaithful with his ex-girlfriend. Crump had been in the house now for more than a month, his friend Robinson for less than a week. And though they didn't know it, their free room and board were coming to an end.

From the mother's point of view, Crump was a kept boy who watched TV by day, hung out with Pilar and her friends at night, slept late in the morning, and then jilted her daughter. Robinson was merely his drug supplier. What was she, a fool? Crump had already been told to leave twice. She hated coming home from work and finding Pilar and him together and Robinson smoking marijuana in some other corner of the house.

She ordered Pilar to give Crump and Robinson one hour to get their things and leave.

"Mom," Pilar said, "you don't know Amir like I do. He has no place to go."

"Let his record producer take him in," the mother shot back. "You go tell the both of them: 'One hour, good-bye.'"

12:50 p.m.

Paul Gambini walked into Southwest Command to pick up his back mail. An old friend of Henry's—they once had worked together as officers—Paul had recently switched offices and now was based at an outlying station. The truth was, he wanted to see Henry as much as get his mail.

They went all the way back to Las Vegas High, when Paul was a sophomore and Henry was a senior. Their paths had crossed again when they worked together in patrol. And they had stayed in touch, playing basketball and golfing together, with Paul visiting Henry's house a few times.

"Hey, man!" Paul said, popping his head into Henry's office.

"Whoa, what's up?" Henry shot back. "I see where your name's on the sergeant's list!"

It was a big thing making sergeant. You commanded a group of patrol officers rather than being out in the squad car yourself. Not only was it a nice hop in salary, it was predictably safer. Usually the ones on patrol dealt with the most vicious criminals and the most volatile incidents. The sergeants were supervisors and rarely got out to the scene of a crime.

"You been playing much golf?" Paul asked, changing the subject.

"Like all the time, bro. I even got Dawn out over the weekend. Some guys and me are going down to the Phoenix Open tomorrow. It's really cool. I know some people who can get us into the hospitality tents."

"You look slimmed down—" Paul started to say, but Henry put up his hand, cutting him off.

He saw that a message was coming in over his scanner. It was a hot call. "Priority alert," it said. "417, Sam5…2Ocean1, 2Sam1, can you be en route?"

As Henry took in the message, his cell rang. It was Dawn, returning a voicemail he had left earlier.

"Can't talk now," he said, his voice clipped and serious. "I'll get you later."

Henry knew that "417" meant domestic violence. "Sam5" was the city sector that included Feather Duster Court, a twenty-five-minute drive from the station under normal conditions. "2Ocean1" and "2Sam1" were the call signals of two of his officers, Bo Neal and Jason Palmieri.

Henry walked quickly to his squad car and waved goodbye to Paul. As soon as he got behind the wheel, Metro dispatched a follow-up message. A man was beating a woman with a stick in the front yard of a house, and breaking windows in both a car and the house. Henry turned on his flashing lights and siren. Twenty-five minutes? *Forget that*, he thought, *I can make it in ten.*

Jason Hansen, who had been at the morning briefing, was eating lunch in his squad car behind a Carl's Jr. Hearing the same message, he knew he was just three major intersections away from the site of the incident. His adrenaline surged. He put the pedal to the floor.

1:12 p.m.

A Metro police chopper hovered above 8336 Feather Duster, its propellers whacking the air and kicking up dust.

The copilot reported by radio that two men and two women were out front, arguing. The women—Pilar and her mother, Engracia—jumped into their new black Chrysler, as if to flee. One of the men, Crump, threw a rock through the windshield, then dashed into the house. The other, Robinson, ran toward the open end of Feather Duster, a cul-de-sac with about five houses on either side.

Palmieri was first into the street, pulling up to the women as they were about to drive away. They were emotional, almost incoherent. They wanted Crump arrested, but the front door was closed. Palmieri quizzed them, trying to make sense of the scene.

Within seconds, Jason pulled to a halt at the foot of Feather Duster a few hundred feet away, his lights still flashing. He stopped and questioned Robinson, then began patting him down. Jason had just ordered him into the back of his car and locked the door when Henry wheeled by and raced up Feather Duster to join Palmieri.

Jason reached for his radio and called in a Code 444: *Emergency. Officers in life or death situation. Need immediate assistance.*

The chopper, hovering above, continued to radio a running account. Homeowners opened their doors a crack and took in the commotion.

As soon as Henry arrived, he jumped from his car. The blades of the chopper made a racket above. His Bible was open on his front seat.

Oddly, the front door of 8336 was now ajar. Had it blown open? Had Crump just turned the knob from inside and allowed it to gradually swing open, setting a trap?

Henry did not take cover but instead walked toward the open door, calling over his shoulder to Palmieri.

"Come on, let's go," he shouted.

"Sarge," Palmieri said, "the guy's still inside!"

Henry's gun was in his holster. He wore no flak jacket. What was he thinking? Was he oblivious to the danger?

He walked as if he were on a mission. It was just like him—proactive, confrontational. He went through the doorway and into a tiny foyer for an instant. The house seemed empty and oddly underfurnished. A stairway led to the second story, with a pony wall adjacent to the steps. Henry turned to go back outside, and the instant he did, a burst of shots came from behind the upstairs wall.

Boom, boom, boom, boom, boom!

One shot struck Henry in the upper back and entered one of his lungs. Its force propelled him forward into a wall. Another shot hit him in the lower back and instantly took out his legs. Two other rounds clipped him, and their momentum carried him through the doorway. He collapsed on his back a few feet down the sidewalk.

"Officer down!!" the cop in the chopper radioed in. "Officer down!! Code 444, officer down!!"

For a moment all was quiet but for the chopper hovering overhead. It was as if Crump and the cops had taken one long, pregnant breath..

Then, another series of staccato shots—*boom, boom, boom, boom, boom!*

Jason, six hundred feet down the street, recognized the sound. It was from a machine gun. Crump was firing with his AK-47 from the second floor in the direction of Palmieri, now crouched with the women behind his car.

It resembled a scene from the war film *Blackhawk Down*. You could hear the fusillade by radio, and on Feather Duster everyone was desperate for cover. All was chaotic.

Seconds after the firing started, it ceased. Henry was still alive but motionless, prone on the sidewalk and losing blood fast. A white haze of smoke drifted and there were odd scenes, almost like mirages. Were those shards of glass protruding with curtains from the front upstairs windows? Yes. All around Feather Duster families had shut their doors or were now hiding behind walls.

Other cops had come up Feather Duster and, hearing the shots, taken cover along the garage door of the house adjacent to 8336. Jason, who had only his forty-millimeter handgun, joined them. They were twenty-five feet from the front door of 8336, which was visible just past a bush if you poked your head around the corner.

Jason wound up closest to the corner. Stealing quick glances, he watched the wounded officer trying to sit up. The man was glassy-eyed, and from a distance Jason didn't recognize him. Henry looked down toward the street and then toward the house. It was obvious he was disoriented.

Suddenly Crump appeared just inside the doorway. *Boom, boom!* A quick burst of shots at the police. *Boom! Boom! Boom!* He had come down to have it out with the cops, who had taken cover behind their cars. Windows were shattering and stucco was flying off walls and houses.

Crump spotted Henry sitting up a few feet down the walk. He stepped twice, pointed the AK-47 close to Henry's head and fired, execution style, killing him instantly. Then he fired toward the police and civilians pinned down in the street. The officers fired back, peppering the front of the house and the doorway with bullets, but Crump retreated inside to reload.

Less than a minute later he was back outside, unprotected, firing yet another fusillade. Crump was staging a twisted climax, as if he would prove himself in death.

Jason and some other officers rushed him, racing across the crushed stones between the houses and firing continuously. Crump went down to one knee and returned the barrage.

In the torrent of shots, one of Jason's rounds jammed Crump's machine gun. Seconds later another shot—maybe Jason's as well—found Crump's neck, exiting from his back and effectively killing him.

It was surreal when the shooting stopped. One hundred and five shots had been fired in a few minutes' time. The acrid smoke had barely lifted.

Jason handcuffed the dying Crump. Another officer went to his car, retrieved a yellow blanket, and placed it over Henry's head. Jason still didn't know who the fallen cop was. He went to look at the nametag on the officer's chest. "PRENDES," it read.

Jason thought, *I can't believe this—this is Henry, who shook my hand only a few days ago and said, "Welcome to the squad."*

Who can fathom the mind of God or comprehend His ways?

Vegas police receive some sixty thousand calls a year involving domestic violence. Yet Henry Prendes was the first Metro officer killed in the line of duty in eighteen years. His death transfixed the city.

In the days afterward, friends and coworkers began to

examine a short list of "what ifs"—as if what ifs could some-how bring Henry back.

What if Henry had stayed in the stationhouse?

Sergeants generally do not answer Code 417 calls. Racing to the scene of domestic disturbances is usually the duty of patrol officers.

What if Henry had been off that Wednesday?

Henry's off days had been Monday through Wednesday. Only two weeks before were they changed to Saturday through Monday.

What if Henry had gone to lunch?

That morning Ted Buchman asked Henry to join him for lunch a few hours later. Henry often lunched with friends. But this time he said no, he'd had a big breakfast.

What if Henry had remembered to bring his bow to work?

His high school friend Pedro wanted them to take their hunting bows to a repair shop just after noon to get ready for a trip they had been planning.

Any one of these scenarios could have saved Henry Prendes's life. Yet God seemingly walked him up to that awful door.

On the evening of February 2, the day after the shooting, more than twenty people showed up at Dawn's home for one of Henry's regular small group meetings. One of the ones who came was Ted Buchman, the man Henry prayed for on the golf course, the guy who said good-bye by shaking Henry's hand. "You need to become a regular," Henry had told him. And this emotional night was a start.

Everyone there had heard the news through phone calls, through friends, via TV—in Dawn's case, while picking up her niece from school. A Metro "police employee assistance" coun-selor had driven up and asked her to get into his car.

Another who was present at Dawn's home was Jason

Hansen, who could say, "There but for the grace of God..."

He told everyone how it happened, and afterward they prayed.

February 7, 2006, dawned cool and bright in Vegas, the midwinter temperature rising throughout the morning to form one of those crisp, gloriously sunny days for which the valley is known.

The funeral procession moved south from downtown the full length of the Strip. Motorcycle officers rode two abreast, the long, solemn line stretching for miles. Henry's coffin, shrouded by the American flag, was borne by a pickup truck.

Uniformed officers stood at attention for two hours on every highway overpass. No one spoke. Live TV feeds on the major stations carried the procession and church service without interruption. Over 150,000 viewers watched in their homes and offices. Outside the hotels and casinos, Vegas stood unusually still.

Typically, Henry left no stone unturned.

He had once mentioned to Dawn that should he die on duty, he wanted the service to be about living. And in a nod to his life-changing trip with Uncle Art to Woodleaf, he wanted to use any contributions for one purpose only—to establish an evangelical camp for disadvantaged or troubled kids.

Four thousand mourners squeezed into Central for the service, and nearly two thousand watched on video screens outside in the parking lots. One of those inside was Jason, so many emotions playing in his heart and mind. The funeral was about to turn into an unusual rite—a celebration and an invitation.

Pastor Jud picked up the Bible that had been on Henry's

car seat. He turned to the Book of John and read: "Jesus said…, 'I am the resurrection and the life. He who believes in me will live, even though he dies; and whoever lives and believes in me will never die.'[20]

"For Henry those words were not just a pie-in-the-sky thought—that was a reality," he continued. "And so he wanted us to celebrate today because he knew with all of his heart that when he left this world he would be with God… "

Dawn took the stage: "Henry had words of wisdom for everyone he met. He had no unfinished business—" she thought of how her husband was persistent to the point of being annoying. "He did what he needed to do on earth and did it now."

Then his fifteen-year-old daughter, Brooke: "I love Christ more than I did my father. And if you want that type of eternal relationship with God, then He will save you; and you too can be your own hero, just like my father."

The pastor added, "Henry would tell you today to leave no doubt about where you stand with your friends and family, leave no doubt about where you stand in your relationship with God.

"And what I know today is this, that if I were to tell you only about the faith that Henry had without giving you an opportunity to experience that same forgiveness and that same faith, that someday when I meet Henry in heaven, he'd come up to me and say, 'Man, you let me down.'

"And I'm not about to let Henry down."

His voice broke.

"Henry today would tell you that the first step is to realize that we've been separated from God by our sin and that God calls on all of us to turn back to Him and do a 180," he continued. "He'd tell you that we need to respond to the solution that God has for this separation. And that we respond by placing our faith and our trust in Jesus Christ."

He talked about the mandate Henry had given him, how the family had commissioned him.

"So leave no doubt," he said. "It may be today for me, it may be today for you, it may be tomorrow. None of us knows when our time will come. So let's leave no doubt today."

He asked those assembled to bow their heads to respect the privacy of others. Then he asked each one who had prayed for salvation to put a hand in the air—an acknowledgement of a decision made.

Around the large auditorium and in overflow spaces, hundreds of people raised their hands. Among the ones who were there was Jason Hanson. The day after Henry was killed, when Dawn had held their weekly Bible study in the midst of her grieving, he had shown up. And on that night he invited Christ into his life. He resolved to live for God, as Henry-the-role-model had before him.

Now, seated in the huge worship center with so many of his fellow officers, Jason thought about the astronomical odds against what had happened... *Here I'm a kid whose family knows Henry...who Henry helps get a health club job...who follows Henry in becoming a cop...who winds up in Henry's stationhouse the week before...who sees Henry again on the fateful morning...who finds himself by chance in the same shootout...who apparently kills the man who has just killed Henry.*

It's much more than coincidence, he thought.

And then to hear about the many lives Henry Prendes touched. How many had Jason influenced?

"If it had been me who fell, they couldn't have thought of more than two or three nice things to say about me," Jason recalls thinking. "I started questioning myself—am I living life to the fullest? For me, the road to recovery started there.

"I'm not scared when I'm on duty anymore—I'll gladly give my life for my job or my country. I'm closer to my wife, my little boy, and my parents now. Life is too short not to be."

As Dawn reflected after Henry's death, it all came down to this: It was as if Satan had walked her husband, God's soldier, to the devil's door, only to have God bring an army to Himself.

CHAPTER THIRTEEN

Amazed

S ergeant Henry Prendes's memorial service was the greatest
testimony to the message of God's grace in the history of Las
Vegas," one lifelong Vegas resident told me. Words don't do
justice to the events surrounding Henry's life and death.
Hundreds of thousands of people were talking about Henry,
the faith of his wife, Dawn, and daughters, Kylee and Brooke,
and Jesus—all in Vegas.

I climbed into a police car after the funeral as the processional made its way to the graveside. While we entered the
freeway near the church, the networks talked about the
Prendeses' faith. They spoke of Henry's wife's strength and of his
daughters' maturity. One TV-news anchor interviewed a pastor
about what it meant to be a Christian. Another read from our
church's website and shared how Central was a church for those
who had drifted from faith or were seeking faith.

As the media coverage continued with live shots from helicopters, I was awed by what I witnessed on the ground.
People lined the bridges along the freeway, placing their hands
over their hearts. Construction workers left work, walked to
the freeway, and saluted. I remember vividly one father and
son holding a large American flag as they saluted. A sign that

hung over a bridge read, "Henry: A Hero in Life and Death." When we exited the freeway and turned toward the cemetery more people lined the streets—moms with kids in strollers, families, and the elderly sitting in lawn chairs. Metro Sheriff Bill Young said he'd never seen anything like it in his thirty years with the police. It felt as if the whole city had stopped. My only frame of reference was the days everywhere in America after 9/11.

At the graveside I was told the processional stretched all the way back to the church, over twelve miles, with vehicles still trying to get out of the church parking lot. It's estimated it would have extended fourteen miles long had there been enough room.

I took my place behind Henry's casket. Taps were played along with a twenty-one-gun salute. Three helicopters flew over in formation and Henry's call letters were used for the last time. After the ceremony, I invited those who wanted to pay tribute to form a single-file line to the casket. For almost two hours hundreds of officers filed by while saluting, making the sign of the cross, and even kissing the casket. Their faces are still etched in my mind. They honored a hero and confronted the hard reality of their life and work.

Dawn Prendes believes God led Henry through that door because He knew Amir, in his own free will, would kill someone. God allowed it to be Henry because he was ready, and his story would spread God's fame in a significant way. She trusts the Bible's promise that "in all things God works for the good of those who love him, who have been called according to his purpose" (Romans 8:28). It does not say everything that happens is good, but God works everything for good for those who follow Him.

Sometimes this is hard to understand. I stand in a hospital room with a young mother dying of cancer and wonder how this can ever work for good. I meet with a family whose son has drowned and question whether something good can result from this tragic accident. I see the Prendes family and know the pain of loss is so real. Is the good that comes out of this better than the pain? Is God's definition of good different from mine?

Over the years I've had to learn to trust even when things don't make sense. One of Henry's favorite passages in the Bible was: "Trust in the LORD with all your heart and lean not on your own understanding" (Proverbs 3:5–6). I may not always understand *why* something happens, but I have learned to trust *what* the ultimate outcome will be—goodness. After all the amazing life-turnarounds I've witnessed in this city, I couldn't believe anything else. God works in our lives for our ultimate good, which means that one day all of His working behind the scenes will bring everyone and everything together under Jesus (Ephesians 1:10).

After the graveside I rode back to the church with the sheriff and a couple of officers. Our thoughts were with Dawn and the entire Prendes family. So many in our community pulled together to help with the memorial. Our church staff and volunteers had done an amazing job. We had seen God "working for the good" of so many. We had coordinated one of the largest funerals in the history of Nevada, said good-bye to a friend, and presented the message of God's grace to hundreds of thousands—more than I ever could have believed was possible when we drove across the desert back in 2003.

Recently, my kindergarten-aged daughter said, "Dad, I know why we moved to Las Vegas."

"Why?" I asked.

"Because God told us to. And because some people might not know who God is, and we want to help them know Him better."

I couldn't have said it any better. It's not that we have all the answers or think we are better than anyone else. We simply believe that God has the answers and that we are loved so much by Him. God's love is deeper, higher, and wider than any unloveliness in our lives. Henry Prendes's life and death prove this to me beyond a shadow of a doubt.

People had been riveted to the media coverage of Henry's memorial service in homes, hospitals, restaurants, hotels, and casinos across town. Entire office suites streamed the service online as workers watched from their desks. In the weeks afterward, our phones at Central rang off the hook and our mailboxes filled with stories of people opening their hearts to God. Many stopped by the church to receive Christ into their lives. Hundreds were baptized. I couldn't keep up with all the stories. We were part of something larger than us, something huge that God was doing in Vegas. We still sense this in a tangible way each day, and I'm constantly reminded of the lessons Vegas has taught me—and is still teaching me—through Henry's death and a hundred other miracles.

I'm reminded that *new beginnings are possible for everyone*. After Henry's funeral, one woman called to say that she had prayed for her husband to come to faith for twenty years. As they watched the coverage of the memorial service together at work, she noticed that tears ran down his face. Afterward he turned to her and asked her to pray with him to make Jesus the leader of his life. One guy e-mailed a story about someone praying to follow Jesus in a dentist's office. Dozens told of spiritual experiences in their living rooms while they watched the coverage.

No matter where you are or what you've done or where you come from, there is hope. I knew this before moving to Vegas, but now I know it at a deeper level. God is available to you in everyday life. As you reach out to Him, He will respond. He doesn't want to judge you; He wants to forgive you and help you begin again.

I've also discovered that *it's okay to not be okay.* Everyone goes through good times and bad. Nobody is perfect. When you fail, you can be honest about your mistakes with God and others. When you hurt, you can admit it. If you are angry with God or you doubt, you don't have to fake it and pretend. God is big enough to handle the truth and so are others. Being honest about your pain, struggles, and failures helps others realize they are not alone in their problems. So many people gathered together on the day Henry was laid to rest, and they found strength and hope in each other. Healing can be found together.

In Vegas, I've seen that *life-change really can happen*. Those far from God can return to Him, including some from other faiths, like thirty-two-year-old Jason Venniro. Jason was a longtime friend of Dawn's and a practicing Muslim. Seeing the faith of Dawn and her family, he was deeply touched. Eventually he returned to the Christian faith and was rebaptized as a follower of Jesus.[21]

Another soul that changed because of the Prendes's witness was Cheryl Williams. Cheryl, a thirty-six-year-old Metro officer who was friends with Henry in the police academy, was searching for meaning in the loss. Moved by watching Dawn and the family, she said: "I could tell that their strength was getting them through this, while I was literally sick to my stomach that my friend isn't here, that he was taken from us. I said to myself, *They know something I don't*."[22] She went on to place her faith in Christ, be baptized, and become the host of a small group Bible study in her home.

Shortly before he died, Henry told Dawn he wanted to find a way to tell more people about God. He wanted to get the message out to the world. Tragically and amazingly, it was his death that took the message to so many people.

Now, several months after the funeral, I'm still stopped regularly and thanked for the memorial service. Last week a woman who didn't know Henry started to cry as she said thanks. Henry's friends and coworkers, as well as those who never knew him, are still coming to faith in amazing numbers. Who would have ever predicted that an officer's death would inspire such life change for people?

Dawn Prendes has spoken to thousands of people over the past number of months. From high school assemblies to golf tournaments to memorials, she has continued to challenge people to surrender their lives to Christ. Before 160,000 NASCAR fans at the Las Vegas Speedway she said, "I want to leave you with words from a song so appropriate for NASCAR fans, when you are running low on faith, throw your hands up in the air and say, 'Jesus take the wheel, 'cause I can't do this on my own.'" Dawn has done this in her own life and God has sustained her on the road.

As more and more turn to God and receive His grace in Vegas, He is writing a story that could someday inspire the nations. People in Mexico City, Sydney, Paris, London, Beijing, Tokyo, and beyond may yet marvel at God's move in the world's most unlikely city. God's fame is changing individuals, families, and neighborhoods. His light is shining in the darkness. Just being a small part of it humbles and surprises me. I often sit back in amazement that God would allow my family to be part of what He is doing in the world.

The afternoon of Henry's funeral, as I thought about all this, I noticed something in the Bible I had never seen before. In Joshua the Israelites roamed the desert for forty years before God led them to the Jordan River to cross into the Promised Land. Over one million Israelites had waited their entire adult lives for this moment. Joshua told the people to prepare to cross, but the Jordon was at flood stage. At any other time of year they could have waded across, but now the Jordan was a raging river.

The Bible says that when the priests walked into the river, "the water from upstream stopped flowing. It piled up in a heap a great distance away, at a town called Adam" (Joshua 3:16). The Israelites were able to cross, but I never noticed that the water piled "upstream" at a town called Adam, which is roughly nineteen miles from where they stood. They didn't even see the miracle. God had already been working upstream in their lives. He piled the water up before they ever stepped out in faith.[23]

When word came of Henry's death, many could only see the raging water. There were so many questions and plenty of frustration. There still is. But now at least we partially see how God worked upstream in the situation. He took tragedy and brought much good from it. He was working even when we couldn't see it.

Sometimes we find ourselves facing raging waters, and we are not sure where to turn. We hear the word "cancer." We lose a job. Our family splits. We feel discouraged. Looking around for God we only see problems. When life doesn't make sense, when we can't figure out what God is doing, when everything seems to be falling apart, trust that God is working upstream in your life. He was working upstream in mine, using my rebellious days to prepare me for ministering to the suffering in Vegas. I know from experience that God sees a bigger picture and works for your good and mine, long before we even realize He's doing it.

This was reaffirmed to me again recently when I met Bebe, a delightfully spunky eighty-year-old woman. She gave me a big hug and said, "Jud, I have been lost for eighty years of my life, and thanks to Henry Prendes I have just now found my way!" As she watched the memorial service, she opened her heart to God and experienced His uncensored grace. When Dawn Prendes heard about Bebe, she sought her out one weekend at Central. There were tears as they hugged. I just stood back and watched them interact for a moment. It was clear that in all the pain God is still working upstream. Good is still to come from our loss. Lives are still to be changed. There is reason to have hope. All I could do was fight back my own tears and whisper thanks to God.

The stories you've read are only the tip of the iceberg. They are happening every day all around the world, as people receive God's grace and live in it. At each moment people from every walk of life are experiencing change. Some are reconciling bitter rivalries. Others are offering forgiveness for the first time or laying down drugs for the last time. And faith is being taken up instead. Tears of pain and joy are flowing as someone gets honest about his or her failures and receives forgiveness.

It is a revolution. And by reaching out to God, you can be part of it...even now. Through God's power and grace, you can become the person He desires you to be. If it can happen in Vegas, it can happen anywhere!

Acknowledgments

Bill and I would like to thank the many people who shared their lives and stories with us for this book. They have been an inspiration to us in every way. We'd also like to thank the team at Multnomah for their partnership and help, especially our editors, David Kopp and Adrienne Spain. Thanks to Chris Ferebee for your friendship, effort, and excellence.

Thanks to the Central Christian Church family for being an amazing community of people. It is such an honor to serve with you. Thanks to Gene Appel for your encouragement. To Mike Bodine, thanks for being a tremendous ministry partner and working tirelessly to help others in so many ways. Your leadership is key in creating the culture we've written about, where so many lives are touched. A special shout out to the Central staff. The difference you make in people's lives on a daily basis is incalculable. Only God knows the full extent of your work. You rock!

Much love to the many awesome communities of faith in Las Vegas. Particularly, I'm thankful to Kevin Odor and Canyon Ridge, and Shane Philip and The Crossing.

Thanks to Paramount Terrace, where I first learned of this grace that has changed my life, and to Tommy Politz for your friendship. To Barry McMurtrie and Crossroads, thanks for modeling a community built on grace. To Mike Foster and Peter McGowan, your friendship and support mean the world to me. Thanks to Gabe Lyons and the Relevate community for the vision and inspiration.

To my wife, Lori, and to Emma and Ethan, thanks for the margin to work on this project and for the times when you pulled me away for more important things—like playing "Duck Duck Goose" in the backyard.

Bill is especially grateful to Donna and Will for their patience, encouragement, and support.

And thanks to God for changing our lives in such a tangible way and for making grace so amazing.

Discussion Guide

I believe that no matter what people have done or where they have been, God's grace is available to them. Through His grace, they can find healing, face addictions, experience forgiveness, see marriages restored, and have their lives changed for the better.

I also believe that church should be a place where it's okay to not be okay, a place where people don't have to fake perfection. People don't have to pretend to have it together. They can come as they are, with their pain, challenges, and junk.

God promises to meet people where they are and begin a work of transformation in their lives. I've seen it happen over and over again.

And so I hope you will approach your group discussion of *Uncensored Grace* in a spirit of openness and expectancy. Bring your life with all its faults to God, share honestly with the others in your discussion group…and see what God's grace will do!

Lookin' up,
Jud Wilhite

SESSION ONE: **GRACE CITY**

Read chapters 1 through 4 of *Uncensored Grace*.

Opening Thoughts

• *Uncensored Grace* author Jud Wilhite is a conservative Christian pastor and family man who was stunned to find God calling him to serve in America's most notorious city: Las Vegas, Nevada.

> What's your first reaction to the idea of Las Vegas offering a model of how God works in people's lives?

• "Like it or not," says Wilhite, "America is looking more like Vegas every day" (page 19).

> How is the place where you live starting to resemble Las Vegas?

• The authors define "uncensored grace" this way:

> Uncensored grace is what you get from a loving God when all the religious types have gone home, and every last hope for your own effort has blown up in your face. Uncensored means that there is no formula or membership or performance that stands between you

and God's goodness. Uncensored means that as wide and deep and high as your mountain of personal ruin might get, God's transforming grace is always wider and deeper and higher (pages 19–20).

Thinking about that definition…
What (if anything) makes you want to stand up and cheer?

What (if anything) makes you uncomfortable?

• What are you hoping to get out of reading and studying this book? (Check one or both.)

___ I want to find out how to get some uncensored grace for myself.

___ I want to learn how to offer uncensored grace to others.

Explain your choice.

Story Chapter Recaps

CHAPTER 2: Stephanie Keene and Donte Harrison are natural-born entertainers. Neither planned on getting into exotic dancing, but that's where their careers took them. And both are among the most popular dancers in Las Vegas's adult entertainment industry. Here's something else: both are believers in Jesus Christ. They learned about Jesus at church, committed their lives to Him, and are trying to live for Him the best they know how. Now married, they are hoping to get out of adult entertainment and start new careers.

CHAPTER 3: Las Vegas has a way of attracting people who are running away from something. Sonny McKenna was running away from a troubled life in California, where his history was one of broken relationships, heroin use, drug selling, and jail time. For him, bass fishing was one of the few pure delights he enjoyed—and he became an expert at it. But in Vegas he continued his spiral down toward homelessness and hopeless drug addiction. Finally, when he was at rock bottom, he learned about Jesus, and his life turned around. Today he is married, sober, and involved in a ministry to help the homeless.

• When you first read about Stephanie Keene's striptease act—and in the next sentence read that she was a born-again Christian (page 25)—what was your reaction?

• For you, what is the most powerful evidence of God's activity in the lives of Keene, Harrison, and McKenna?

• One big reason that these three people met Jesus is that they encountered a church where they were welcomed despite not even coming close to fitting the stereotype of a got-it-all-together Christian.

What's your reaction to people like these when you meet them? Honestly, are you more loving or more judgmental?

If you've ever been a part of loving someone into a relationship with Jesus—someone who was morally or spiritually objectionable—tell about it.

Personal Application

• Wilhite confesses to having gone through a "spiritual wrestling match" when faced with the paradox of people in the adult entertainment business who love Jesus (page 61).

Have you ever gone through a spiritual wrestling match when dealing with people who have messy lives but who profess to love Jesus? If so, describe it.

• Speaking about his adopted hometown, Wilhite says, "While the world may see this area as Sin City, I see something else. I see a place where grace is found and shared, where new life is experienced, where relationships are healed and hope is born. I see a city filled with people God loves" (page 61). In other words, he sees it as Grace City.

Have you ever had a vision of your town or city as a place where God would do amazing things in the lives of desperate people? If so, tell about it.

As you seek to see a vision like that become a reality, what would it look like for you to "err on the side of grace," as Wilhite puts it (page 62)?

• Jesus held out both truth and grace to the people He met. Read John 8:10–11 for an example.

Comparing yourself to Jesus, what part of His example do you feel you need to copy more faithfully, and why?

• The authors are concerned about the number of loveless churches in our country—churches that fail to offer uncensored grace.

How would you say that your church is doing at showing love and grace to people who have messy, unattractive lives?

Your Chance for Uncensored Grace

The authors say, "Every day is an opportunity for a new beginning. Every day there is hope because of God's grace" (page 67). That means *today* is a chance for you start fresh.

Choose one or both.

A	B
If you have never accepted God's grace for salvation, accept it today. Jesus knows your sin and its awfulness better than you do, but He loves you anyway and wants to enter into a relationship with you. He wants to start changing your life for the better. So if you believe that He is the Son of God and that He died on the cross to take care of your sin problem, confess your sin and ask Him to come into your life. He will.	Spend some time in prayer asking God to bring to your mind one spiritually needy person to whom He would like you to offer uncensored grace. Write that person's name here: _____ 　　As you are working through this study of Uncensored Grace, be looking for ways to share the compassion and forgiveness of Jesus with this person.

SESSION TWO: **GRACE TO BE**

Read chapters 5 through 8 of *Uncensored Grace*.

Opening Thoughts

- How happy are you with who you are? Check one.

  ___ Hey, everybody should have it as together as
  I do.
  ___ I'm not perfect, but I'm content with who I am,
  and I'm not looking to make any changes.
  ___ I've already seen some changes for the better
  taking place in my life, and I expect to see some
  more.
  ___ I'll admit it: there's a lot I'd like to change about
  myself if I could.

- Do you believe people can change—not just superficially
but in fundamental ways? Why or why not?

- When you think about changes you'd like to see in your
life, what comes to mind first?

Story Chapter Recaps

CHAPTER 5: Jason Walters was more idle than "idol." He had no job and was hanging out at his sister's place in the Caribbean, mostly smoking pot, when he got a chance to try out for the hit TV show *American Idol*. Out of thousands of would-be contestants, he made it into the top sixty before getting cut. After this, Jason returned home to Vegas, where an old girlfriend invited him to church and he became a believer. The next time he tried out for *American Idol*—and got cut again—he realized that his life's purpose lay not in fame but in God. And he'd already found it.

CHAPTER 6: What could be more Vegas than skydiving Elvises? Brian Balducci, point man for the Flying Elvi, was a tough guy who thrived in the risky business of jumping out of airplanes and making pinpoint landings for others' entertainment. But in his personal life, his relationships with women were a tale of one failure after another. Finally he found his way to church and to Jesus. Brian has since quit working with the Flying Elvi, and today he is happier than ever. With God in it, his life is no longer "Heartbreak Hotel."

CHAPTER 7: Chris Gunderson, just eighteen years old, had become a Christian a few years earlier but had since drifted away from God, getting caught up in drinking and drugs. Then youth leader Drew Bodine, by "coincidence," crossed paths with Chris when the young man needed some help and inspired him to recommit himself to God. It was a shock to Drew and to others when Chris died in a one-car accident a few days later. His return to the Lord had come just in time.

- What changes did God's uncensored grace bring into the lives of these three men?

    Changes in Jason Walters's life:

    Changes in Brian Balducci's life:

    Changes in Chris Gunderson's life:

- Which of these three stories touched you the most and why?

Personal Application

- In chapter 8 Jud Wilhite tells how he tried and failed to conquer his drug addiction. It was only when he turned to God that he was delivered. As he says, "When we've done so many things wrong, we need God's help to believe our lives can ever be made right again" (page 125).

    How has God changed you in the past?

What hope do those past changes give you for
the future?

• Even after we've become believers in Jesus and have begun
to be changed by God, we can bear a heavy load of guilt and
failure that drags down our view of ourselves.

What messages of self-hatred do you hear in your
head (things like, "You're no good," or, "You'll never
amount to anything")?

• Wilhite found freedom from his own self-hatred when he
realized that "what *God* thinks of me matters infinitely more
than what *I* think of me" (page 126). He recognized that,
because he was made in the image of God, he had value and
dignity. He was already loved by God, and all he had to do
was to embrace God's grace.

Has the meaning of God's grace ever struck home
to you so powerfully that it changed your view of
yourself? If so, describe what that was like.

Would you say that embracing God's grace is something we have to do only once or that we need to
choose it over and over again? Why?

• God's grace is free, but it comes with a responsibility: to try to live holy lives and to seek God's forgiveness when we fail.

Right now, what do you need to ask God's forgiveness for so that you can go on as a man or woman who lives in uncensored grace?

Your Chance for Uncensored Grace

"God can give you the ability to reimagine your life and dream again" (page 131). Believe it? You should. Read 2 Corinthians 5:17.

Chapter 8 mentions two exercises that people have used to try to reimagine their lives in the light of God's grace. Choose one or the other to do for yourself. But whichever you choose, spend some time in prayer first, asking God to give you *His* vision of your life.

A	B
On one part of a sheet of paper, put down words or images that represent your life now. On a differen part, put down other words or images to represent the life you think God wants you to have in the future through His grace. (See page 129 for an example.)	Find a small rock. Hold it in your hand as you think about the sins you have committed and the burdens you carry. Pray for God's forgiveness and for Him to work a revolution in your life. Then go outside to a safe area and throw the rock as far away from yourself as you can. (See page 131.)

SESSION THREE: **GRACE TO BELONG**

Read chapters 9 through 11 of *Uncensored Grace*.

Opening Thoughts

• What's your gut reaction when you hear the word *church*?

___ love	___ tedium
___ loathing	___ disappointment
___ fear	___ warmth
___ gratitude	___ pride
___ shame	___ anger
___ detachment	___ other:_____

• Do you think most people view church as a place to find a "family" and a sense of belonging? Why or why not?

• Looking inward, do you detect a need within yourself to be part of a loving community? If so, how strong is that need, and how does it reveal itself?

Story Chapter Recaps

CHAPTER 9: Geoff Sage, a numbers guy, rode the up-and-coming Aspen Creek gaming company to wealth as an executive—

and then lost his job in a corporate merger. Geoff first began praying to Jesus when he needed help handling the stress in his life. In time he gave his heart to Christ, and today he is the treasurer and chief operating officer for a church.

CHAPTER 10: Scott Reader was formerly a successful designer within the cosmetics industry. After years of living the lifestyle expected in the upper level of New York's homosexual community, Scott lost his job, lost his money, and lost his lover. Suffering from AIDS, he moved to Vegas. And there (to everyone's surprise but God's) he found community in a church, turning his life and his lifestyle over to Christ.

• If Geoff had showed up at your church when he was still an unbeliever and working as an exec for a purveyor of slot machines, would you have wanted him to become a part of your church community?

How about if Scott had showed up at your church when he was still an unbeliever, a drug user, and a practicing homosexual?

What's behind these presumed reactions?

- What amazes you most about the uncensored grace seen in Geoff's life? In Scott's life?

Personal Application

- Summarize the history of your relationship with the church. What Christian bodies have you been a part of and why?

When have you chosen to separate yourself from church and why?

How do you feel about church now and why?

- When have you most felt a sense of belonging with other followers of Jesus?

When have you felt most rejected by the church?

• The authors argue that God has a dream of community for His people—a dream that becomes a reality in the church.

> Try to put yourself in God's position for a minute. Why do you think it is important *to Him* that the church be a place of belonging?

• In chapter 11, Jud Wilhite admits that the church is messy because it is filled with imperfect people. Then he chides, "But let's get over it and get on with helping people experience God's grace" (page 173).

> What, if anything, is holding you back from "getting over" the church's flaws and "getting on" with helping people?

• Wilhite argues that a shift has occurred in our society so that now people often connect with a church body first and only later trust in Jesus and start living more godly lives (page 173).

Old pattern	New pattern
1. Believe	1. Belong
2. Behave	2. Believe
3. Belong	3. Behave

> Do you agree with Wilhite that this change has taken place?

On the whole, is it a good thing or a bad thing? Why?

How have you seen a new Christian (perhaps even yourself) follow the belong > believe > behave pattern?

• Speaking of his church, Wilhite says, "We do not water down the Bible or the teachings of Christ, but we do accommodate in every other way possible. We love people no matter where they are" (page 174).

> Consider your own church. Is your church weak either at holding onto the truths of the Bible or at welcoming sinners into its community? What's your evidence for this assessment?

• How could your church do a better job at being a place of belonging for people at all stages on their spiritual journeys?

• The overwhelming attitude that Jesus had toward unbelievers was compassion. (See Luke 13:34 for a glimpse of His yearning for the lost.) And as the authors say on page 176, Jesus' example should cause us to question ourselves: *"Do I have the compassion of Jesus for those who are hurting or disillusioned? Is that compassion evident to others?"*

How would you answer?

Your Chance for Uncensored Grace

Choose one. (And for the time being, forget about what you think *others* ought to be doing. This is about *you*.)

A	B
If you've been hanging back from getting involved with other Christians... What steps will you take to join a community of Jesus followers and find the belonging that both you want and God wants for you?	*If you are already part of a Christian community...* What will you do to welcome others—regardless of their beliefs or lifestyle— into your community and help them find a sense of belonging?

SESSION FOUR: **AMAZING GRACE**

Read chapters 12 and 13 of *Uncensored Grace*.

Opening Thoughts

• How has your view of yourself changed over the course of reading and discussing *Uncensored Grace*?

How has your view of God's grace changed?

• What's the most important thing you've learned from reading this book?

• In what area of your life do you presently feel the greatest need for God's grace?

• Right now, how much of a sense of expectancy do you have that God will work miracles of grace in your life and in the lives around you? Mark a spot on the continuum below that indicates your attitude.

Never happen here   *Why not here?*

●━━━━━━━━━━━━━━━━━━━━━━━━━━━━━━━━●

Story Chapter Recap

CHAPTER 12: Henry Prendes was a Las Vegas police sergeant, family man, and outspoken Christian. Then on February 1, 2006, when a domestic violence call came in, Henry went to the scene and strode fearlessly into the house. Within minutes he was dead from multiple gunshot wounds. What was most amazing was the response to this officer's death. The thousands who honored him at his funeral heard a powerful message of the gospel, and hundreds chose to follow the same Lord that Henry did.

• As you read the story of Henry Prendes, what amazed you the most about his life or death? What amazed you the most about the reaction to his death by others?

• Taking into account the "what ifs" that might have prevented Henry's death, the authors comment, "God seemingly walked him up to that awful door" (page 198).

    Where was God in Henry Prendes's death? Where was grace?

Personal Application

• Commenting on the powerful Christian testimony that arose from Sergeant Prendes's death, Wilhite says it is an example of God taking something bad and turning it into something good.

> As you think about the bad things in your life, how might our grace-filled God bring something good out of them?

• The Prendes experience reminded Wilhite of three truths:
1. New beginnings are possible for everyone.
2. It's okay to not be okay.
3. Life-change really can happen.
   > Which of these three truths do you most need to take to heart and why?

• Referring to the priests crossing the Jordan River in Joshua's day, the authors point out that God must have been working upstream to dam the river—even before the priests took their "step of faith" into the water.

> Think about an area of need in your life. How might God be working "upstream" in your life to prepare for a work of grace? How does it make you feel to know that might be happening?

- Two exotic dancers (Stephanie Keene and Donte Harrison). A homeless heroin addict (Sonny McKenna). A pot-smoking would-be "American idol" (Jason Walters). A skydiving Elvis impersonator (Brian Balducci). An eighteen-year-old backslider (Chris Gunderson). An out-of-work gambling company executive (Geoff Sage). A homosexual dying of AIDS (Scott Reader). A police sergeant killed in the line of duty (Henry Prendes). These are some of the people God has singled out to receive His grace in "Sin City."

The authors proclaim, "If it can happen in Vegas, it can happen anywhere!" (page 210).

> What do you hope to see God do in your town or city?

> Are you starting to see it happen? If so, what's the evidence?

Your Chance for Uncensored Grace

Read Ephesians 3:20–21. Then choose one or both of the options below.

A	B
Think one more time about an area of your life where you are in need of grace. You have probably been praying about this need for some time. But are you *believing* that God will give you grace for it?	The revolution of grace that is taking place in Las Vegas is one that can spread anywhere—even to your town.
Find a Scripture verse that gives you confidence that God will do great things for you. Before God, pray an "I believe, help my unbelief" type of prayer (see Mark 9:24). Start trusting that God, in His time (always the right time) and in His way (always the best way), will bless and change you.	Commit to praying and working toward that end until you see God doing amazing things in the lives of people around you. Write your commitment on a sheet of paper in the form of a "manifesto of uncensored grace" stating in bold, straightforward terms what you are intending to do. Keep your manifesto someplace visible in your home or workplace as a reminder of your determination.

Your Group's Chance for Uncensored Grace

It's great to read and discuss a book that talks about the amazing grace God is working in others' lives. It's a great *start*, that is. But do you know what is much, much better than that? *Actually being a part of what God is doing.*

What would you think about your *discussion* group turning into an *action* group? Together, pray and decide how God might want to use you to work His uncensored grace into the lives of people in your own "Sin City." And then go for it. As a team, you can accomplish so much more than any individual could do.

Endnotes

1. Neil Postman, quoted in Marc Cooper, *The Last Honest Place in America: Paradise and Perdition in the New Las Vegas* (New York: Nation Books, 2004), 12.
2. Joel Stein, "The Strip Is Back," *Time*, July 26, 2004.
3. Ibid.
4. Friedrich Nietzsche, quoted in Andrew Stirling's sermon "Luther—the Radical," Timothy Eaton Memorial Church, October 29, 2000, http://www.temc.net/cgi-bin/ms2/temc/bbs/sermons-1/date/63.
5. D. A. Carson, *New Bible Commentary: 21st Century Edition*, edited by D. Guthrie and J. A. Motyer. (Downers Grove: Inter-Varsity Press: 1994), in Logos Bible Software: Scholars Addition.
6. See F. F. Bruce, *Paul: Apostle of the Heart Set Free* (Grand Rapids: Eerdmans, 2000), 250.
7. J. Murphy-O'Connor, "Corinth," *The Anchor Bible Dictionary*, Vol. I. (New York: Doubleday, 1992), 1135–1136.
8. Ibid.
9. Ibid., 1138.
10. Hal Rothman, *Neon Metropolis: How Las Vegas Started the Twenty-First Century* (New York: Routledge Press, 2003), 61.
11. *Life*, March 20, 1970.
12. Elvis Presley, quoted in Greg Laurie, *Life. Any Questions?: Finding Spiritual Meaning on the Fast Track* (Dallas: Word, 1995), 17.
13. Bono, quoted in Michka Assayas, *Bono in Conversation with Michka Assayas* (New York: Riverhead Books, 2005), 203–204.
14. Dawn Haglund, quoted in Robert Webber, *The Younger*

Evangelicals: Facing the Challenges of the New World (Grand Rapids: Baker, 2002), 48. Dawn states the older paradigm was behave, believe, and then belong. I alter this order, as belief has been more primary than behaving in my experience of twentieth-century evangelicalism.

15. Thomas Cahill, *The Desire for the Everlasting Hills: The World Before and After Jesus* (New York: Doubleday, 1999), 156.
16. Thanks to John Ortberg for this insight.
17. This was in an unpublished paper and study done by George Barna for Gabe Lyons and the Relevate community.
18. Thanks to Grant Fishbrooke for this phrase.
19. See Cahill, *The Desire for the Everlasting Hills*, 246–248.
20. John 11:25–26
21. Cheryl Williams, quoted in Christina Littlefield, "Reaffirming Faith," *Las Vegas Sun* (March 25, 2006), www.lasvegassun.com/sunbin/stories/text/2006/mar/25/566649331.html.
22. Ibid.
23. See Brian Jones, *Second Guessing God: Hanging on When You Can't See His Plan* (Cincinnati: Standard Publishing, 2006), 34–35.

About the Authors

The author of *Uncensored Grace,* Jud Wilhite serves as senior pastor of Central Christian Church in Las Vegas. Thousands of people attend Central's campuses each weekend, along with a global community who attend online. A frequent conference speaker, Jud co-authored *Deadly Viper Character Assassins* with Mike Foster. He and his wife, Lori, have two children and a slobbering bulldog.

Bill Taaffe is a writer and editor whose articles have appeared in *The New York Times, The Washington Post,* and *Sports Illustrated,* where he was a columnist and senior editor for nearly ten years. He and his wife, Donna, live in the Las Vegas area with their son.

For more information on the revolution of grace, check out:
www.uncensoredgrace.com